Paul Pryor In His Own Words:

The Life and Times Of A 20-Year Major League Umpire

By
Fred Pryor
With Gary Livacari
March, 2018

ISBN: 9781980742319

Library of Congress Control Number:

Amazon Direct Publishing Platform

Printed in USA

Copies of this book may be purchased at Amazon.com

Dedication

Big Pops: I am so happy to make your vision come true! I hope this book makes you proud, as I am so proud to be your son. I could have not had a better father, teacher, coach & advisor throughout my life.

Big Moms: Truly this book should celebrate your life, as you are the real heroine of this story. Raising four children on your own for over six months a year with no male presence is nothing short of amazing. We never missed a meal, always had clean clothes and generally had all we needed to live a good life. I know that was incredibly difficult on you and took its toll over the years. Words cannot describe my admiration and love for you. You were, in fact, the Original Big Red Machine!

Tricia: The REAL ROCK and INSPIRATION of the Pryor Family! All of my love and thanks for everything you have done, and do for "Our Tribe". You are the one!

Paul and Sam: Big Pops was so proud to be your grandfather. He loved both of you so very much! I hope you enjoy his stories.

Melanie: I love you! In memoriam RIP Ross and Patrick.

Gary: Without your love of baseball, this book would have not been possible! Thank you very, very much. You have my highest compliments sir!

Contents

Paul Pryor Photo Gallery

All photos from the Pryor family personal collection

Foreword

I first made the acquaintance of Fred Pryor, son of Paul Pryor, back in December, 2016 when he contacted me through my Facebook page, *Old-Time Baseball Photos*. As part of my editing responsibilities, I often interview descendants of former major league players. I then write a detailed post about the player with the personal input from the relative and feature it on my Facebook page. Until that time, I had never interviewed a descendant of a former umpire. Fred and I emailed back and forth about his dad; and I then wrote an interesting Facebook post about him which was well-received by my readers.

As a long-time Cub fan who started on his sixty-plus-year love affair with baseball back in the mid-1950s, I was well aware of Fred's dad, the late former major league umpire, Paul Pryor. Paul was an outstanding, well-respected National League arbiter for 21 years (1961-1981). I didn't consider him one of the "old school" umpires I remembered from my youth like Augie Donatelli, Tony Venson, Ed Sudol, Chris Pelakoudas, and Al Barlick. I remembered Paul Pryor as, to me, a "younger generation" umpire, making his major league debut in 1961.

As I wrote that Facebook post, I learned a lot about Paul Pryor, who Fred had described to me as "one of a kind." Once, when I asked about his dad's upbringing and whether he was "outgoing" in his youth, Fred made a revealing reply: "I don't think he had a shy bone in his body." As I was to learn later, truer words were never spoken.

A year later, Fred contacted me again, this time asking if I would be interested in helping to edit a biography of his dad. I responded that I most certainly would be. As we discussed how we would approach the project, Fred informed me he had in his possession approximately 160 pages of notes written by his father during his career. Fred remembered that when his dad was on the road, he would often record tapes about the game of baseball and also about his life as a major league umpire. His dad had mentioned the notes to Fred before his passing in 1995, but Fred had never seen them until after his mother died in 2000. At that time, Fred stumbled upon them in a box in his parent's garage. Fred made copies of the papers, and suggested that I look through them. Possibly they would be of some value for our project. He also expressed the hope that perhaps I could make some "rhyme or reason to the madness." I said I would try.

When I received the package, I realized these were more than just "notes." I perceived immediately that I had a treasure-trove of first-hand information in my hands. They were written by a man who had lived and breathed baseball from "inside the white lines." These were nothing less than Paul Pryor's personal memoirs – his life story – complete with ongoing, detailed commentary on the "passing scene": baseball as it existed from the1940s through the 1980s.

A large part of the collection was devoted to his reflections on the often exciting life of a major league umpire. Exciting, yes… but oftentimes equally lonely and depressing. It's a profession where lack of respect from fans, players, managers, front offices, and even commissioners was a given fact of life. Combined with a daily pressure-packed existence where your every mistake is on display, often before a national audience; a grueling 162-game schedule with unending, physically-exhausting travel; where impending physical injury awaits with every pitch. Throw in six months each year away from your loved-ones, where absences from important family milestones are an accepted part of the job description, and it's amazing anyone would ever choose to enter such a profession – much less survive in it for twenty years. Yet Paul Pryor did just that; and what's more, he made it abundantly clear that he loved his life as an umpire. Somehow he looked upon it as the best job in the world.

Other topics covered in this cornucopia of information included the vast difference between an umpire's life in the majors as compared to the minors; the many characters Paul had met in the game; comments on the game's stars; the many memorable games in which he was involved, including personal reflections on three the World Series; umpire colleagues; and even managers. This list just scratches the surfaces of the topics covered. The papers were surprisingly well written and edited; and I realized immediately that this was a story waiting to be told. Thus Paul Pryor's personal memoirs became the genesis of our book: *Paul Pryor In His Own Words: The Life and Times of a 20-Year Major League Umpire.*

Not only was Paul Pryor an outstanding umpire blessed with a keen sense of observation, he was not afraid to make critical commentary about the game he loved. No one was off limits, including players and managers. Nor did baseball commissioners go unscathed. With his discerning eye, Paul Pryor was often able to penetrate deeper into their personalities, much deeper than the superficial veneers they often presented to the public.

Fred Pryor is understandably proud of his dad, who he fondly refers to as "Big Pops." Over his career, the Woonsocket, Rhode Island native umpired 3,094 major league games, including three World Series, four League Championship series, and three All-Star games. Pryor's crew had many memorable games, including one on May 31, 1964 that went 23 innings. The second game of a double header, it's the longest doubleheader in National League history. They also called Jim Bunning's Perfect Game on June 21, 1964, one of only 23 official Perfect Games in major league history.

A respected umpire known to have a "thick skin," Paul Pryor recorded only 30 ejections over his career, including one stretch of nearly five years without a single one. He was very familiar with the hazards of the game, once suffering broken teeth from a Willie Stargell foul ball that caught him square in the mask. Pryor maintained his teaching and coaching positions during the off-seasons, and worked at various times as a car salesman, a football referee, and even a beer salesman. He retired from umpiring in 1981 after on-going struggles with foot problems.

Paul Pryor was also an accomplished public speaker, and later, became a successful business man. In the 1970's, he designed a duffel bag for umpire equipment. The idea caught on, and soon "Paul Pryor Travel Bags" were on the market. At one time the company had accounts with the NCAA, Major League Baseball, the National Football League, the Canadian Football League, plus many schools and businesses.

In addition to his success as an umpire and in the business world, Paul Pryor was a devoted husband and father of four. He tried hard to balance all the many demands placed upon his personal life by a career that kept him away from home six months each year. Like most American families, the Pryor family was not without its share of tragedy: A daughter, Paula Ross Pryor, died in a car accident in 1979; and a son, Patrick John Pryor, was found murdered in 2001. Fred recently made contact with another sister, Melanie Renee, after a very long absence.

Fred summed up for me his relationship with his dad: "We were like all father and sons: Have fun, laugh, goof off, and yes….clash & argue a few times along the way." Paul Pryor, affectionately known to his family as "Big Pops," passed away on December 15, 1995, aged 68, while residing in St. Petersburg, Florida.

I hope you'll enjoy the story of his life, written in his own words: *Paul Pryor In His Own Words: The Life and Times of a 20-Year Major League Umpire.*

Gary Livacari

Park Ridge, Illinois

January, 2018 Home

Introduction

My father, Paul Pryor, was a man of many talents. First and foremost, he's remembered as one of the most highly regarded umpires in major league history, having officiated 3,094 major league games over a 21-year career (1961-1982). This included three World Series, four league championship series, and three All-Star games.

He was also a great athlete in his youth, starring in baseball and basketball during his high school years. He later logged many years as a minor league pitcher and umpire, some, as you will discover, under the most trying of circumstances. In addition, he was an accomplished and highly sought after banquet speaker; an outstanding writer and teacher; and a successful entrepreneur and businessman. But most important, he remained a devoted husband and father, whose family's well-being was always first and foremost in his mind.

In spite of all his accomplishments, my father never lost his sense of humility. Throughout his life, as his successes accumulated and advanced him onto the national stage, he remained the same "humble guy" who hailed from the small mill town of Woonsocket, Rhode Island. He "never forgot his roots," and always remained the loving father our family fondly referred to as "Big Pops."

I often observed him interacting with others. The way he treated the clubhouse attendants, grounds crew personnel, cops, firemen, parking lot attendants, and even bar tenders left its impression on me. Everyone was treated with dignity and respect. He had come from very little, so he spoke their language and knew their daily struggle. He made it abundantly clear to me the value of the "everyday person." In his opinion, the guys that get up each and every day and go to work to provide for their families were the ones who were the "real heroes." The guys who had perseverance and grit – those were the ones to be admired and emulated.

What you are reading is the story of his life, written in his own words in his own unique style, amply supplemented with heavy doses of his brand of self-deprecating humor. As you read along, you'll discover his unyielding determination to fulfill his dreams of reaching the major leagues, a dream that found him traveling from city to city over many years in the grueling minor league circuit. He never gave up, facing and overcoming obstacles that would have stopped many an ordinary man.

But Big Pops was no ordinary guy. Once injury ended his hopes of pitching in the majors, he decided to try his hand at umpiring on the very day he was cut from his last minor league team. To top it off, it was something he had never even tried before. But true to form, when Big Pops did something, he gave it his all. As it turned out, it just happened to be a great fit... and the rest, as they say, is history. He had found his niche in umpiring; and through hard work and sheer determination, he steadily advanced through the minor leagues until that day late in the 1961 season when he finally "got the call." He had fulfilled his life-long dream of reaching the majors – not as a pitcher, but as an umpire.

After my father passed away in 1995, my mother told me dad had been recording old baseball and sports stories on a small voice recorder while driving between1981 and 1985. His intention was to someday write a book which would retell his experiences both in life and in baseball. He hired a local student to transcribe them on to manuscripts; and then kept the papers stored in his garage. My mother passed away in 2000, and as I was going through my parent's belongings, I discovered an old cardboard box full of papers tucked away in a corner of the garage. The box was in bad condition from years of exposure to the Florida humidity.

At first, I had no idea what was in the box. Then I recalled my mother telling me about dad's book project. I loaded the box into the moving van and transported it back to my home in Texas. I at first made a cursory read through the papers, but they sat undisturbed for many years until my own retirement in 2013. Out of curiosity one day, I pulled them out and began rereading, this time a bit more intently. I soon realized I had uncovered a real treasure trove: this was my dad's book project, his personal reflections on life, his upbringing, and on his many years umpiring in the major leagues.

It dawned on me that his stories were ones that needed to be told. Who else besides me would be the one to tell them? I found myself mesmerized by the first-hand accounts of his early life, his successes and travails in the minor leagues, and his subsequent rise to become a highly respected National League umpire. I also thought there would be many baseball fans who would enjoy reading these personal accounts of "life between the white lines" as well. That thought back in 2013 gave birth to the publishing project you now have in your hands. In 2016, I made the acquaintance of author Gary Livacari. We began to discuss the possibility of a book based upon my father's memoirs, as well as other recollections from my life growing up as a son of a major league umpire.

As Paul Pryor's son, I was extremely fortunate to have many great thrills – ones that sometimes left my friends a little envious. I had the opportunity to visit umpires' locker rooms, plus time in numerous major league dugouts and clubhouses. With Big Pops having contacts throughout the entire sports world, I was even able to visit NFL clubhouses and locker rooms. Over the years, I met some of the most famous athletes and sports personalities in the country.

In 1981, after 20 years of service as an umpire in the National League, my father retired due to recurring foot problems. Retired, yes...but stopping? No, not at all! He immediately immersed himself in the company he had purchased in the late 1970's: the Paul Pryor Travel Bag Company. Over time in his new career, he established nationwide accounts with MLB, NCAA, NAIA, high school athletic teams, and businesses across the country. His company manufactured sports travel equipment bags he himself had designed, as well as numerous other sporting goods accessories. In his capacity of owner and chief promoter, he spent hours traveling in his van visiting schools and sports' teams. In addition, at this time of his life, he became an accomplished and highly-sought banquet speaker, with an ability to "speak off the cuff," eagerly regaling tales from his 21 years in the major leagues, including first-hand stories about the many sports celebrities he had met.

Big Pops could fit into any environment. He was very comfortable in his own skin. True to his humble origins, he would always make himself the brunt of the joke if need be in order to get a laugh or get people involved. Dad always told me he didn't care what I did in life, but whatever path I chose, do it to the best of my ability. "If you do a job, do it right…the first time," he always said, "don't come back for seconds!"

I leaned many life lessons from my father: How to always have unyielding determination in pursuit of your goals, to never give up no matter what obstacles life may deal you. I learned the importance of keeping yourself grounded, to never forget your roots, and to never let success go to your head.

As an example of how he "practiced what he preached," I used to hate coming home after church when I was a kid because I was required by my parents to hang up my Sunday clothes. Of course I was in a hurry to get out and play. Therefore, my suit usually got hung up in haphazard fashion. Well, that drove Big Pops nuts! He would always say: "If you do it right the first time, no one can find fault with you!" Fortunately for me, the lesson eventually sunk in!

Most importantly, I learned invaluable lessons on how to treat others. It's a cherished philosophy passed down from my father to me and now on to my own children. It's summed up beautifully in this, my favorite Paul Pryor quote:

"Everyone has value, everyone matters. Never treat someone any better just because he makes more money or has an important title. Everyone counts. There are no exceptions. There are no ordinary people."

That's Big Pops in a nutshell…and he unashamedly lived his life in accordance with this maxim until his dying day.

My father, Paul Pryor, a special man of many talents and accomplishments who always remained a devoted husband and father, passed away on December 15, 1995. It's my intention to honor his memory by preserving many of his stories and reflections upon life, retold in this book and written in his own words. I hope you enjoy them as much as I do.

Fred Pryor
Bedford, Texas
January, 2018 Home

CHAPTER ONE

THE UMPIRES NEW CLOTHES

"I hear you're Paul Pryor's son, huh? I knew your old man when I played ball back in South Dakota, back in the late '40's or so. He was a helluva guy…"

The voice that accompanied the static telephone line sounded like national league president Warren Giles, but I couldn't be sure. Whoever was playing the Senior Circuit Chief had to be a smooth practical joker because I couldn't hear any stifled chuckles in the background.

I granted a few intelligible "yeses" and "nos" and waited for the caller to make a fateful slip. League presidents do not make a habit of calling their umpires just to shoot the breeze. Usually a personal call with small talk was only his prelude to shouting a litany of mean metaphors.

The voice continued without breaking into laughter. I thought that maybe Augie Donatelli or Eddie Vargo had recruited a guy who sounded like Mr. Giles and then wrote a convincing script for him to follow.

I was just about ready to laugh and say," Okay, buddy, put the umpire next to you on the phone. Nice try, in fact, you're damn good. You really had me going…" When the voice suddenly sounded awfully realistic. Mr. Giles wanted to know if I was

1

interested in becoming a member of the National League umpire delegation to the 1967 World Series.

"Are you kidding?" I asked him.

He explained that I was one of three National League umpires he held selected for Series honors. I hemmed and hawed nervously a few times in my best Ralph Kramden invitation and finally said, "yes, yes, yes!!"

I'm sure that we both examined the receiver suspiciously before hanging up. Whether Warren Giles was serious about making me a member of the World Series crew or he had heard about my own telephone stunts and decided to play a practical joke on me.

A telephone in the hands of some umpires could be more lethal than a bat in the grip of Hank Aaron. I had a phone routine devised for road trips that was designed to either make me a candidate for the Comedian of the Year Award or send me reeling into the emergency room with a broken jaw.

Umpire Bruce Froemming carried a buzzer in his pockets that he activated when a likely prey was within range. He'd let his pockets sound off for a few long moments while I opened my brief case and spoke into a portable telephone. The trick was to be sure we at least knew the first name of the subject on the joke and that he heard Bruce's buzzer. This was especially great fun on planes because flight attendants and conventioneers frequently wore some sort of identification on their lapels.

Once when Froemming and I worked a Pirate series in Pittsburgh toward the end of one season, our little prank nearly cause a full-scale riot in the bar of the Roosevelt Hotel. It seemed as if the entire squad of Steelers was seated in the lounge when Froemming's buzzer and my telephone were working overtime. Players were being paged to my phone quicker than lines changing after a fumble.

Huge men who barely qualified to be Cro-Magnons lumbered up to my telephone for their calls. Froemming and I laughed uncontrollably at some of their reactions. A few guys were actually so embarrassed at not hearing another voice over the line that they invented brief conversations. Others scowled at me as if they were prepared to make me a part of the carpet. By the time I packed up my briefcase, most of the Steelers had made their pilgrimages to my phone. Some players hung around the bar hoping the important caller would try again. Others were so jaded that they couldn't even bother to answer the hotels pages over the intercom.

I decided as I sat by the phone after Warren Giles' call that no one, not even a league president would be so heartless as to invite an umpire to officiate a World Series under false pretenses. Whether he knew about my telephone antics or not, I felt sure that he decided to include me in the National League's delegation.

It was a thrill for me to umpire every game during the course of a long season, but umpiring in a World Series is in a category all its own. Even beyond the professional esteem of being selected to umpire a Series, it is baseball's crowning ceremony, a time when the sports fanfare and panache are on festive display. People who are not even fans take the time to pay attention to the baseball season's grand finale. Radios and portable televisions suddenly find their way into schools and workplaces.

The action is recorded in the minds of millions of fans, so that in hindsight, the blur of some distant season and all its faces and plays and nuances are somehow recalled by the winner and loser of the World Series. Besides, fans for years and years to come would see me on television in the baseball clips Mel Allen made especially for rainouts.

I had been in baseball a lifetime before I was even assigned to umpire the1967 World Series. I played professional baseball in the minor league systems of the St. Louis Cardinals and the New York Yankees. After they told me they loved me and that I had a lot promise – promise in something other than the majors, I shuffled around the lower echelons of the minor leagues' bumdom. I never blamed my releases on any lack of interest. I was just short in the talent department. Nearly everything baseball could offer in a lifetime except success as a big league player seemed to have come my way. I sported a beard to play with a bunch of Bedouin tribesmen on an itinerant pro team called the House of David; I managed in the Basin League of the woolly Dakotas and instructed hockey players how to drop their bats after hitting when I managed in Canada's Laurentian League. Following a stiff sentence of ten years as a minor league umpire, I was finally, miraculously, and thankfully called to the majors in 1961.

After six full seasons and some seventeen-odd games later, I received my call from National League President Warren Giles and became a part of the 1967 World Series umpiring crew. But what made the occasion even sweeter was when I discovered my crew pal Augie Donatelli was also going to be a member of the National League's detachment. I knew I was going to have fun. Augie was a member of my original crew in 1961 and he took the extra time to show me some of the ropes of the big parks and was a great friend. I knew if the Boston fans decided to suddenly bathe me in beer or throttle me with the blunt ends of their Fenway franks, Augie would at least be there to console me.

The 1967 World Series proved to be a great matchup between the Red Sox and Cardinals. It was my first time as an official in any American League park. My turn behind the plate came in the fateful sixth game in Fenway Park. I'm told my escapade that day will be enshrined in the Baseball Hall of Fame when that long-awaited wing called the Home for the Terminally Confused is finally erected.

I arrived at Fenway Park three full hours before the start of the game. This is going to be my big moment calling balls and strikes in a World Series and I itched with excitement. There were six umpires assigned to the games, but only four separate crates of equipment arrived at the stadium. Two guys would have to put on dark suits and look like futile funeral directors for the game.

Umpires' equipment is customarily forwarded from city to city by a railway or airline freight express company. The great majority of the time the equipment arrives well in advance of the game and saves any member of the crew coming down with a sudden attack of the Don Knotts' Syndrome.

Normally I would have thought this was funny but when I discovered that my crate and Ed Runge's of the American League where the missing ones, I narrowly escaped a conniption fit. How in the name of Leo Durocher was I supposed to work home plate duty without any of my equipment or uniform? There I was, ready for my big day in Fenway Park during the Series with the eyes of the baseball world focused on me while my entire equipment locker was sitting on someone's porch in Paducah, Kentucky, or Moscow, Idaho.

No matter what happened, I had to go out on the field even if I was dressed like a refugee. But there was a delicate problem in borrowing parts of the other guys' uniforms. I'm 6'2" and weighed 230 pounds at the time. No one else in the crew was built like a sofa.

I had a severe case of the screaming mee-mees as they danced around the locker room trying to borrow bits and pieces of a passable uniform. We put our heads together and the results was a cornucopia of clothing. The outfit we finally concocted made me look like an ad for a fire suit sale after the first cleaning.

I used Augie Donatelli's mask, Johnny Stevens' shin guards, God knows whose indicator, while Al Barlick personalized my wardrobe by loaning me his protector and supporter. I also borrowed his blue jacket which was shy about three inches in each sleeve and road way up my Southern exposure. But the wardrobe's crowning glory were the pants and shoes. Frank Umont of the American League was the only umpire with a spare pair of both. The problem was that Frank was 5'10" tall and wore size 9 ½ shoes. The gunboats I normally wear are size 12.

The other guys just watched with horror and surprise as I crammed myself into the new uniform. I felt like a giant in elf's garb. This was the way Li'l Abner was supposed to look when he officiated games in Dog Patch. On top of all this, Frank's pants had a bum zipper. There was absolutely no way I could put on the pants and zip them up.

When I finally walked onto the field, some of the fans in the front rows thought I had taken a nasty fall. The players were convinced I let a Boston wino dress me that day. I felt so small I could have sat on home plate and dangled my legs. My only hope from real disaster was a safety pin holding the zipper together, more or less. Sometimes it would pop open and I'd find myself looking down at a sharp, shiny object sticking out of my zipper. Unfortunately, the sun was shining and it made the pin glitter like a diamond tiara. Real class.

The late, great Elston Howard caught that Series for the Red Sox. In order to adequately call balls and strikes when Elston was behind the plate I had to accommodate my stance to his, crouching in such a way that my safety pin and Elston's cushion were in close proximity. Several times the pin popped loose and Elson would jump from his position, rub his derrière and say, "Hey, what are you doing? Is my rear supposed to be a pin cushion or something?" Other times, he would rise in one startled jolt and rub his bottom thoughtfully.

To make matters worse and even more painful, the sixth game of this Series turned out to be the longest. For three hours and 45 minutes my size 12 feet lost three inches of bragging rights in Frank's size 9 ½ shoes. As soon as the game was over and the Red Sox won 8-6 to carry the Series to a seventh game, I dashed to the umpires' locker room, took off the vices on my feet and made an emergency call to a podiatrist.

National League President Warren Giles made a trip to the dressing rooms to chat with the umpires. He congratulated me on calling a good game and took a hard, close look at me. "Don't we give you enough money to buy uniforms?" he asked.

For some bizarre reason, when fans first learned that I spent 20 years in the National League as an umpire, they think the first memories that must come to my mind involved a great players like Musial, Maris, Mays, Clemente, Banks, Koufax, Gibson, Stargell, and Rose. Nothing could be farther from the truth. My most poignant and painful memories on the National League diamonds involve the occasions when I was beaned or careened with bats and fastballs or when I was obliged to take the field completely out of uniform. Excruciating pain and total embarrassment have a way of demanding front row attention from my memories.

Umpires have never been known to dress like Yves St. Laurent or Bill Blass, but their fashions have recently changed for the better. When I broke into the majors in 1961, both players and umpires looked as though they were addressed by Omar the Tentmaker. Players were fashioned in baggy, woolen pajamas and umpires looked like giant box turtles on the field. But with time, the styles became somewhat more streamlined, form-fitting, and less cumbersome. Players now have finely tapered uniforms, almost to designers' perfectibility that allows greater comfort and freedom of movement. Umpires no longer look like cheap funeral directors in baggy garb. The English schoolboy caps with the short rims have been changed to a hat more approximating those of the players.

A fashion craze struck umpires in the 1960s when the leagues decided to put the AL and NL letters on the caps. Heavy materials were substituted with lighter fabrics for the hot summer games. Knowing how to effectively use umpiring equipment and the proper way to dress on the field is as much a part of instruction at umpiring schools as learning the rulebook. But few people, thank God, besides umpires understand the appropriate deportment and trousseau of the trade.

Once in 1967, Jimmy Piersall asked me if he could borrow my equipment and uniforms to umpire and old-timers' game. The idea of Piersall actually umpiring a game seemed like the pinnacle of sacrilege. This was the same character who used to hide behind the monuments in Yankee Stadium between batters. I had the home plate assignment for one game when Jimmy decided to commemorate his hundredth home run by running the bases backwards. The National Pastime would never be the same again after he worked home plate. It was akin to having the criminal wear the judge's robes and preside over the court.

I arranged with Jimmy a time for him to drop by the umpires' locker room to pick up my equipment. In the meantime, I devised a little stunt I knew he would appreciate. By the time he entered the dressing rooms, I was putting the final touches on my scheme.

I felt that if Jimmy was going to play umpire for a day, he should know the proper way to dress the part. I put my equipment and uniforms on him backwards. Everything an umpire is supposed to wear faced south. Shin guards were on the back of his legs, my pants zipped up his rear, my shirt buttoned down his back, my chest protector covered his back, and even my cap was flipped backwards. My supporter and cup would have been on him backwards if it were possible.

Jimmy took a good, hard look at himself in the mirror and asked, "Hey, Paul, how come you got everything on me backwards?"

"For you, I thought this was the best way to show how an umpire is supposed to dress. And besides, by now everyone expects you to do everything ass-end backwards, anyway."

Christmas came early to Veterans Stadium one midsummer day in 1978. I had the home plate assignment for a Phillies game when the umpires' equipment trunks failed to be delivered to the ballpark on time. This is not so much a disarming discovery for the three men assigned to the base duty as it is for the umpire calling balls and strikes behind the plate. They can borrow spare caps from the home team's equipment manager and wear a black or navy blue suit. These guys may look like recent grads from the National Embalming School, but it is a close enough approximation of what they would normally wear on the bases. But the home plate umpire has to be decked in a variety of protective gear and equipment like a tank to avoid embarrassing and untimely trips to the hospital.

When game time approached, I was at the mercy of the good tastes of the Phillies' equipment manager. By the time I was supposed to be at home plate to accept the lineup cards from the managers, I was dressed like Santa's new 230 pound elf. The Phillies managed to acquire the largest pair of home uniform pants they could find. A red towel was haphazardly stitched together by the trainer for a ball bag. I wore the athletic shoes of the Philadelphia coach who had a pair of canoes like me. A loose Phillies' red sweat top, and extra set of catcher's shin pads, an athletic cup and supporter from who knows where, a Philadelphia cap, and thick strips of sponge tape across my toes rounded off my wardrobe. It was a delightful combination of holiday red and white. When I emerged from the Phillies' dugout after this impromptu dressing session, the whole stadium roared with laughter. It was a thoughtful way to remember Emmett Kelly's birthday. Spontaneous outbursts of "Jingle Bells" erupted from all parts of the stands.

Leo Durocher was never short for words when it came to umpires. If he wasn't shouting a tirade of dangling diphthongs from the dugout, he always had a wisecrack to deliver. Beneath that little chrome-dome head, operated a fertile factory of cranks.

I had the first base assignment one day when the umpires' equipment failed to arrive by game time. I put on my navy blue suit, a white shirt, and a black tie and strolled to the base to assume my position looking and feeling like a new priest. As I walked past Leo's dugout, he noticed that I wasn't dressed properly. I knew the creative gears in his mind were working furiously in a crisp comment would soon be delivered.

"Hey, Paul," he called out while I was walking around the first base area.

I looked over to Durocher and waited for the result of his poignant observations. "What in the hell are you supposed to be dressed up like today, a standup comedian?" He asked.

Working a game behind the plate with a makeshift uniform can be embarrassing for an umpire, but most of the time it doesn't physically hurt. Getting smacked with a fastball or a bat hurled like a missile does. Fans have very different opinions about players and umpires injured on the job. A player's injury is regarded as serious – fans don't usually laugh. Even an accident on the field that might appear to be minor could potentially keep a player off the diamonds for the rest of his life.

The fans usually don't mind when an umpire is injured. In fact, frequently they considered that he had it long coming to him. There is a human quality that enjoys to see the official in a precarious situation. The boxing ref that inadvertently gets a haymaker to the head will make the evening news as a comical feature. The cop who trips over a banana peel while pursuing a bunch of delinquent kids is part of stock slapstick humor. The umpire who is beaned in the head with a wild pitch is frequently serenaded from the stands with shouts of "Hit him again! That'll make him get a real job!!"

Human beings are born with 206 bones in their bodies and the average adult has about 32 teeth in his mouth. But after 30 years, the numbers get sufficiently jostled to make a veteran umpire a classroom study for dental and medical students. There are breaks, snaps, creases, crevices in unlikely places, not enough teeth to eat Jell-O, and the awkward dilemma of missing this or that part of your body.

But I was genetically prepared to become a major league umpire. Instead of signing an umpiring contract with the normal number of bones and then recognizing it was all going to be downhill from there, I was biologically engineered for the profession. I was born with an extra bone in my left ankle.

Most people would think that with an extra bone in my ankle that it would accent my athletic abilities. Wrong. The problem is that no one has ever been able to determine what the extra bone is supposed to do. It's never made me dance like Fred Astaire, or beat a delicate bunt to first, or even helped me push off the mound respectfully when I was a pitcher. It's just there. What it does, however, is make me look as though I have a perpetually swollen ankle and it makes buying shoes a colossal problem. But at least when I began umpiring with 207 bones, I knew I had a little leeway for errors.

No umpire can leave 30 years of work without some good dental and osteology stories. It's more than just the risks of the trade. It's an absolute promise that the ball and umpire are going to go thud in the night a few times.

My first major catastrophe occurred in Charlotte, North Carolina, when I was umpiring a Southern Athletic League game in 1960. I was hit with a foul ball that knocked out virtually all of my bottom teeth. I took off my mask and watch helplessly as bits of teeth and blood cascaded into my hands. No sooner did the fans realize I was injured when I heard someone yell out clear and crisp above the noise of the crowd, "It should have killed ya, ya bum!" Real sympathy.

History has an odd way of repeating itself. I had outfitted myself with a set of false teeth. When I was assigned home plate duty, I invariably would leave my lower choppers in cold storage in the umpires' locker room. Then I made one fateful exception to my own rule. I felt courageous after four full years without dental reconstruction and overextended my luck while covering an Atlanta Braves' game in 1964. It was in the terrible fourth inning when I was cold-cocked by a careening foul. The impact dislodged my dental plate and caused a lot of pain, blood, and more pain. I took off my mask and asked the Braves' trainer to return my damaged dentures to the umpires' locker room. No sooner did I return to the action of the game when I heard a fan yell out as clear as the bells of St. Mary's, "It's too bad that pitch didn't kill ya, ya bum!" I was properly fitted with gauze pads and made the remainder of the play calls looking like Don Vito Corleone.

Invariably, when I tell people these stories, their first thoughts run something along these lines – "Paul, did you realize that when you call balls and strikes behind the plate, you're supposed to wear a face mask?", Or "Just because Jerry Ford played football without a helmet, what gives you the right to think you could umpire home plate without a mask?"

People don't realize the Newtonian dynamics of very fast balls in flight. A pitch encountering a bat at 90 M.P.H. is going to leave the bat in acceleration of 90 M.P.H. The meeting of ball and bat causes the ball to increase speed *en profundis*. Hence a ball at 90 M.P.H. driven off the bat will hit my mask as though it was doing a cool Mach 9 in flight. The impact alone on the umpire's mask is sufficient to rearrange certain God-given facial features. I know, I am a case in point.

When I used to tell players, managers and other umpires that I was "hanging my head" every day, it wasn't because I was necessarily ashamed of my umpiring attributes. Willie Stargell hit a foul ball that gave me a case of baseball whiplash. Pittsburgh was playing Los Angeles and it was the Dodger trainer who prescribed a remedy I'll never forget. After a battery of x-rays and examinations were given and it was determined that nothing was bent, twisted, or juxtaposed in my neck, the Dodger trainer gave me a contraption that he must have heard was once used by Theodoric, medieval barber of York. The device was an elongated plastic bag that fitted over a door. My head cozily slipped into a built-in harness on one side of the door, while the counterweight of a water bag hung on the other

14

side. Supposedly, the aches and pains of outrageous fortune would be countermanded by this apparatus.

I was faithful to this bizarre expedition in neck rearranging and spent many a productive hour with my head in a plastic harness and managed to get a jeweler's eye view of the fine woodwork finishing on my floor. But to add insult to injury, I nearly broke my neck in this Rube Goldberg device. The telephone rang suddenly and instead of daintily removing my neck and answering the call, my whole body moved at once with a painful delay between the time my feet went for the phone and my neck stayed on the contraption. So much for the trappings of modern medicine.

Steel-toed shoes are another necessary part of the home plate umpire's arsenal. Objects in flight have the nasty tendency to be directed either at the head or the feet. Low pitches that escape the catcher's clutches, hastily or purposefully flung bats, catchers' masks and hot hot dogs seem to have a natural affinity for the umpires' feet. The problem with steel-toed shoes, however, is that they are not all steel. Just enough metal is built into the shoe to protect the ends of the toes. The leather portion from the base of the toes to the laces just beyond the protective barrier of the steel is a favorite target for low-flying objects. Many times I've danced around home plate with a hot foot while the fans have clapped their favorite accompanying tunes. Once when Frank Robinson played for the Cincinnati Reds, he had a foul ball that made a strategic run for my feet. It hit that vulnerable area just above the steel tip and broke my toe.

But the fait accompli, the coup de grace, the Croix de Guerre, the red badge of courage, as well as the penultimate of ultimate umpiring injuries occurred to me on one bright August afternoon in 1966. This is the sort of accident that sends cold chills up and down the spines of all umpires.

I was assigned to home plate duty in a pitching clash between Bob Gibson of the Cardinals and Sandy Koufax of the Dodgers. Sandy threw an atomic-powered fastball that ricocheted off the dirt and hit me in that small margin of space umpires call "under the protector." I involuntarily performed a swan dive. It was similar to the routine of Artie Johnson on the tricycle in "Laugh In" as he hit the fire hydrant and keeled over. I toppled sideways in the same position as I was hit. It was like turning an upright picture of Paul Pryor umpiring and then positioning it 90° sideways on the turf of Bush Stadium. I was out in a New York second.

I came-to after a few capsules of smelling salts and twenty-four hours later I got Sandy's rendition of the incident. The next day he informed me that two gay men died in the stands when they saw what had happened. But Sandy was always a gentleman and a great sportsman and he apologized on national TV for ruining my anniversary. It was then that I really learned that baseball and high finance do have a few similarities. You've got to protect the family jewels. Home

CHAPTER TWO

THE CARE AND FEEDING OF A YOUNG UMPIRE

"Everyone has value, everyone matters...Everyone counts. There are no exceptions. There are no ordinary people."-Paul Pryor

Woonsocket, Rhode Island, is a small mill city snuggled on the banks of the Blackstone River. It is near the northeast corner of this tiny state and, relatively speaking, little more than a Frank Howard home run away from the Massachusetts border.

Woonsocket was a mill town like dozens of small New England cities from Pawtucket, Fall River, and New Bedford to the Merrimack River towns of Lowell and Lawrence. Red brick mills that produced textile goods and shoes once hummed day and night along the river banks. Raw leather and rough textile materials from across the country arrived by trains and trucks at the mill gates. Factory whistles blew, smokestacks churned, and through the multitude of windows in each mill immigrants and sons of immigrants could be seen day and night operating great machines. Woonsocket was another Middletown whose factories, homes, and lives were clustered behind broad, sleepy rivers. The men and women who filed through the gates of these dingy little mills became the shoemakers and clothiers for a growing nation.

I was born in Woonsocket on July 10, 1927, an only child and unfortunately, I never knew my father. I was an only child and an illegitimate son. My mother worked as a nurse in New York City and traveled every other weekend to Woonsocket to be with me. I was raised in my grandparents' small home with my cousin, Neil. My grandfather worked on the city's trolley cars and my grandmother, Mary Teresa O'Neill worked in one of the textile mills. The kids at school called her "Lint Head" or "Cotton Head" because she worked in the mills and couldn't afford to be a homemaker, at least not on a trolley car worker's salary. But she knew right from wrong and the older I get the more I'm convinced she did a wonderful job raising Paul Pryor.

I grew up in a day and age when good decent blue-collar, hard-working, God-fearing people, despite their frugality, despite the years of work at the mill or trolley lines were undeservedly classified as "the lower class." We were poor, but I never knew that as a kid. We were lucky to have three meals a day, but when we sat around the dinner table, they were great meals

I was never a lonely kid simply because I never had the time to think about being lonely. Sports consumed my time on and off the fields and courts. Big, two-hearted players like Hal Newhouse and "Schoolboy" Rowe were the men I wanted to emulate. These were the grown-ups I thought I was like even as a kid – adult players who disliked to leave the baseball diamond but returned home when the game was over and the lights went out and the fans filed out of the park.

Things seemed simpler than. Baseball was a giant metaphor for the game of Life. There were some days that were rainouts, and others that were wins, losses, walks, strike outs, and even on a lucky day – a grand slam in the ninth inning. The mill town of Woonsocket had changed tremendously since then. The red brick factory buildings are mostly vacant, the mill whistles don't blow anymore at the changing of the shifts, but it was great to be lost on the baseball field there in the middle of July, in the middle of summer, forever.

As a backyard territory of metropolitan Boston, Rhode Island teemed with Braves and Red Sox fans. While my friends religiously followed their favorite players at Braves Field or Fenway Park, I was in love with the Detroit Tigers. Players like Tommy Bridges, Rudy York, Mickey Cochrane, and Hank Greenberg were Titans – larger-than-life men who performed the impossible from my grandparents' radio.

When twilight settled on the local playing fields and my friends returned home to their families and dinner, I took my ball and glove to the cement wall in front of my grandparents' house for my private sessions. Amongst the long shadows of the streetlights, I bounced the ball off the wall and made spectacular plays just like the Tigers. I imitated their infield pick-ups and throws to first. I pitched and Mickey Cochrane caught my strikes and in the shadowy twilight world, I somehow knew all the Tiger players. They were more than heroic characters whose names and deeds crackled from the radio. I somehow knew each man for exactly what he was – heroes who stood head and shoulders above other players on and off the field. Detroit, Michigan, was halfway across the nation from Woonsocket, Rhode Island, but

I knew that my Tiger heroes were decent men who knew right from wrong and if I could become a man like Hank Greenberg, everything would be all right for Paul Pryor.

Although my family was poor, education was given a ranking priority. My mother and grandparents were more than willing to pay the modest tuition and uniform costs to send me to St. Charles, a Catholic parochial school in Woonsocket. After the eighth grade, I moved along the natural parochial route to Mount St. Charles high school and was co-captain of the basketball team and a pitcher and third baseman for the Mounties. Off the school courts and diamonds, I played for several local amateur teams that were so popular in New England at the time.

I pitched for the North End Dodgers along with my friend and classmate Clem Labine, the great Brooklyn and Los Angeles reliever. Clem and I were kind of dynamic duo on and off the field. We were both the same height, both built like bears, and we both wore the same style crewcut. We were both hurlers on the Vin Carney amateur team that won the league championship and I pitched for the Lucy Maderna League down the road in East Providence. During Boston Brave practice sessions, Clem and I threw training to the Braves' pitchers and non-roster players. It was a thrill to throw to the big leaguers, but none of the local glamour ever managed to rub off, I was still a dyed-in-the-wall Tigers fan. An eagle-eyed baseball scout wouldn't have called me a bona fide, certified, "good" pitcher, but I could throw the ball hard.

An incident occurred at Mount St. Charles High School temporarily changed my life and to this day remains a complete mystery to me. I had a schoolboy fight in my senior year with a guy whose father was the editor of the Woonsocket *Call*. A few days after the incident, the poor kid was ambushed on the way to school and "de-pantsed." This was a creative and imaginative source of fun and sometimes retribution at the time that involved stripping someone of their pants. The tricky part was that it was accomplished without the victim knowing who his playful assailants were. In other words, it took a great deal of planning on the part of our fertile young minds to pull off – both the pants and the mystery of our identities.

I don't know whether the guy reported to the priests and brothers half naked or whether he went home through the streets of Woonsocket in BVD's, but he did squeal to the school officials. The Prefect of Students called a 10 o'clock assembly and informed the entire student body – "I have a difficult task to perform, the expulsion of one of our boys." I was *that* boy, but I was totally innocent. I had a fight with the guy only a few days before the stripping scene, but I was the sort of character who confronted my foes toe to toe. I would never have resorted to jumping someone with a couple of comrades to steal a guy's drawers. It was just too low. Despite all my explanations to the contrary and a little begging and pleading, the good priests were convinced I was guilty by default. Decent young citizens and respectable young Christians did not jump fellow students and steal their pants on the city streets. Everyone at Mount St. Charles knew I had a fight with the kid and by the simple process of guilt by association, I automatically became the fall guy.

I made varsity in virtually every sport St. Charles participated in. I was co-captain of a good basketball team and now had to leave the school two weeks before the start of basketball season on a de-pantsing charge I never committed. It hurt to leave St. Charles and travel across town to Woonsocket High School, but I swallowed my pride in one large gulp and joined the archrival student body. My instant alma mater declared that I was ineligible to play on their basketball team for 18 weeks. This was adding insult to injury. But rather than let one of the city's star basketball players remain idle, I was made the new junior varsity coach.

To this day, I cannot return for a visit to Woonsocket without making a few inquiries to the incident. Some of my close high school pals became priests. I thought that if I couldn't get some straight answers from the men of the cloth, then the mystery of the de-pantsing may be buried forever. Whenever I see my clerical chums I keep asking, "Father Walsh, was it you who stole the guys pants? Father Poirier, how about you? Who took those pants, anyway?"

If the perpetrator happens to read this book, I can easily be contacted at my sports luggage company in Clearwater, Florida. After four decades of living a mystery, I feel entitled to some qualified answers. I've also since gained a sense of humor.

With all the amateur leagues, semi-professional teams and small-town minor leagues scattered around New England, it was sometimes difficult for baseball scouts to adequately make the rounds. Everyone wanted to play professional baseball and teams blossomed quicker than dandelions throughout the New England countryside. It was handy if you knew a friend who knew a friend, who, in turn, knew another friend who might know a professional scout.

Clem Labine was the local baseball great. He had a sinker that dropped over the plate like a cannonball off the Grand Canyon. Gus Savaria, our high school coach, knew Roy Sherwood, the owner of the P & Q Clothing Store in Woonsocket. Roy, in turn, was a friend of George Army, the trainer of the Rhode Island Reds hockey team. George, believe it or not, was a friend of Leo Durocher. Through this complex network of communications, George Army was finally able to recommend Clem to the great Durocher.

In those days, there was always the possibility that a good player could get overlooked for the rest of the trees in the forest. Overworked and underpaid scouts hustled between dingy hotels and greasy diners to cover all the small baseball towns. But once Leo Durocher got a chance to see Labine perform in Boston, he was on his way to the pros.

Roy Sherwood, the local clothier, was the closest man to a father I ever had. He took an endearing interest in my many trials and tribulations and gave me the sort of encouragement that made me believe I could someday play in the big parks with the big players in the equally big leagues.

Clem Labine and I joined the pros on the same day in 1945. He signed for $1500 a month and was given a plane ticket to report to the Dodgers' minor league franchise in Virginia. I had to believe at the time that the Dodgers were a real swanky team because I signed with the Cardinals as a pitcher for a paltry $150 a month and was given only a cup of black coffee and a bus ticket to Allentown, Pennsylvania. But I still shivered with excitement over the thought that somebody was going to actually pay me for what I enjoyed most – playing baseball.

DiMaggio and Williams were going to have to move aside just a little because Paul Pryor was going to play professional baseball in Allentown!

As far as pitchers are concerned, there are probably two major categories with a number of sub-classes to each category. But strictly speaking, there are hurlers and finesse men. I belong to the former category, while Clem Labine was a finesse player. That meant he was a good pitcher.

Hurlers are usually bigger, hardier, earthier, and tougher, but probably not brighter than the finesse pitchers. They throw hard but sometimes lack a few of the trade's finer points like control and a variety of pitches. But I could throw as hard as the best of the Neanderthals. The drawbacks of the caveman approach to hurling included frequent soreness, arm burnout, and the tendency for the batter to become quickly accustomed to a limited retinue of pitches. More than frequently, hurlers run the risk of getting clobbered and sent to the showers way ahead of schedule.

I stayed in Allentown long enough for the Cardinal organization to take a good look at me on the mound and decide what exactly they were going to do with me. I soon discovered the Cardinals had really big plans for me – beautiful Johnson City, Tennessee. I never considered this a banishment to baseball's more remote hinterlands because I still thought that getting paid to play ball was the greatest thing since gingersnaps. Some of us just take a little longer to learn, that's all.

I was quickly learning the dance moves to the minor league two-step. The Cards and Johnson City got tired of me and I signed with the Braves to pitch the 1946 season in New England's

Eastern League with the Hartford Chiefs. During spring training, I received a little notice from Uncle Sam's draft board. I went to Fort Devens, Massachusetts, for my physical and was declared 4-F because I had arthritis in both ankles. While the Army wouldn't even allow me to ride shotgun in one of their tanks, I still expected to run on and off the mound as a professional athlete arthritis and all.

I played only a portion of the 1946 spring training season with the Braves' organization before I packed my worn duffel bag and moved on to Portland, Maine. This was an independent franchise and undoubtedly the worst team in the whole wide world of professional baseball. We proved to be the best batting and worst fielding team in the league. Pop flies and slow grounders were harder for us to understand than Chinese algebra. When I tell baseball people that I played on the worst team in the pros, they are usually weary of my assessment. "You mean, even worse than the early Mets, Paul?" Much worse. We couldn't field the ball to save our sporting souls.

Walter Alston managed the Nashua, New Hampshire, club that was on our schedule. Don Newcombe, Roy Campanella, and several other future Boys of Summer were members of that squad. My only saving grace of 1946 occurred when I pitched against Nashua and the future Dodger greats.

For 8 1/3 innings, I pitched a super game. Then something happened. Campy had a base hit followed by a base on balls I delivered to Alston and then two fielding errors. The young Bums of Flatbush beat us 5-4 in a hard fought match, but I took great consolation in having held them from the plate for almost the entire game.

I contacted baseball fever earlier than virtually anyone else I know. I was moving frantically from club to club and to anyone who would sign a guy who got a big kick out of throwing a baseball around. I left Portland at the end of the 1946 season and signed with the Yankees on their Class B Colonial League team in Waterbury, Connecticut. I was just starting to get the point that professional baseball was not exactly crazy about my pitching. Between Allentown, Johnson City, Hartford, Portland, and now Waterbury, I was traveling around more than a door-to-door insurance salesman. But this was the baseball world, or at least what I thought was the baseball world, and you had to put in the time and take your share of the licks before you got the chance to play with the big boys in the big leagues.

I spent only six weeks with the Waterbury Timers before I was given another bus ticket to another new hometown. This time I was bound for the Carolina league in Greensboro, North Carolina, a place I associated with chain gangs, grits and cotton, right in the buckle of the Hookworm Belt. But Greensboro seemed fine to me. With my residential status in the minors, it wouldn't be long before I would be packing my bags again for some other new and exciting midsize city.

Tragedy struck the team on the return trip from a game in Virginia. Our bus was hit by a truck. One of our pitchers was killed in the collision and a number of players were injured. For quite a while after the accident, the team was depleted of both morale and manpower. I played shortstop, third base, and centerfield to fill-in the personnel gaps until the rest of the players were able to report back to work. Once the roster was filled, I returned to the Greensboro Patriots' pitching mound.

It finally dawned on me in Greensboro that perhaps I was becoming a baseball tramp. This is a sub-sub-stratum of American athletes who were caught in the vicious cycle of minor league teams. It was a world where a player could sign immediately after high school and for untold years shuffle around towns and learn nothing more than about the best road houses and the best overland routes between turnpikes. The guy could grow up and grow old in the minors in those days without coming near a major league park. Sometimes you never even stayed in a town long enough for the fans to know you from the program. The bus rides tended to get longer, dinners got greasier, and your hair got a little grayer.

It was the sport's School of Hard Knocks, baseball's Gulag Archipelago for invertebrate hardball bums. The South was as crowded with minor league teams at the time as was the North. Everybody wanted to play professional baseball. Seven separate minor leagues had claims to franchises in North Carolina alone. There was the Coastal Plain League, the Tobacco State League, the Carolina League, the North Carolina State League, the West Carolina League, the Blue Ridge League, and the Tri-State League, without even mentioning the semi-pro and amateur leagues. I realized in Greensboro that a dismal possibility loomed over my head. Conceivably, I could get lost in the Carolina minor league shuffle and not returned to Rhode Island until I was way beyond the age to have children.

My roommate in Greensboro was another pitcher named Jim Foxworth. One day we were hanging around the room talking when Jim noticed a gold-colored basketball amongst my belongings. He asked me about it and I told him it was a trophy I received years before for playing with the All-Tournament semi-professional basketball team in Worcester, Massachusetts. I told him I was the fifth man who played on the tournament team against a squad comprised of such collegiate greats as Bob Cousey and George Kafton of Holy Cross, George McKinnon of St. Anselm's, and Dick Kirby of Trinity College.

With a line-up like that to face, it was important to tell people that I was the fifth man on the team. Each of the five guys on the court has a specific duty to perform in order for a team as a whole to be successful. One player is a good playmaker, one is a good shooter, another is a good defensive man, still another is a good rebounder while the all-important fifth player is the one who is good at getting in other peoples' way on the court. This is a necessary but sometimes futile task, but I was glad to oblige my services. So I was good enough to make the squad but not good enough to star. But I did make my contribution to the championship team and I was proud of playing against Bob Cousey and helping win the tournament for the Whitinsville Plumber Athletic Association.

Jim Foxworth detected that I was getting a little depressed with the minor-league doldrums and told me about Ralph James, the football and basketball coach at High Point College in North Carolina. The minor leagues had no retirement plan for lifers and it began to seem like the right time to look for a real occupation.

Jim was a graduate of High Point and he seemed enthusiastic about the college's sports program. He recommended me to Ralph James as an athletic scholarship candidate. It seemed like a great idea to me at the time. I could get my education paid with scholarship funds, play sports, and maybe acquire some additional credentials besides a laundry list of minor league teams.

Ralph was a great coach and an outstanding human being, but he was more notable throughout the South for having coached Choo-Choo Justice on his old high school football team in Asheville than he was for his four years with me at High Point. I made up my mind in 1948 to become a college man during the off-season and plug along with the minors as long as somebody was going to pay me to play baseball. It was a little like enjoying the best of both worlds.

Because I was an uncontrollable baseball hobo, I just couldn't pass up one last chance to pitch in the Class D Georgia State League before enrolling at High Point in the fall. I left Jim Foxworth and the Carolina League for the burgs of the Peachtree State. As long as a glimmer of hope still existed to play in the big leagues, I was willing to give it a try. Someone, even if it was in the minor of the minor leagues in Georgia was still willing to pay me for playing baseball. But by this time, I was beginning to get the distinct impression that this was not exactly the way Bobby Feller and Joe DiMaggio reached the majors.

I didn't even get a chance to show the Georgians my best pitching form that season before an arm injury sent me to the showers for good. But I couldn't see missing out on the sport just because I was cut from the minors, so I pursued the big leagues in my own way. I became an umpire the very night I was released as a player from the Georgia State League.

Steve Summerfield was an umpire in the League who was involved in an auto accident the same day in 1948 when I was told by the team to take a long, long hike. I called Jody Matt, the athletic director of Middle Georgia College and league president to ask if he had found a replacement for Steve. He said that he hadn't and then asked the magic question – "Have you ever umpired before?"

"Are you kidding? Oh, sure!" I lied. "I've umpired before."

It seemed reasonable that since I'd logged so much time on the baseball diamonds, I should know how umpires worked. After all, the hard part was playing the game. The umpires were the guys dressed like undertakers who called balls and strikes and out. What could be so difficult about that?

Right after my big lie to get the job, I raced to an Army-Navy store to try to put together the accoutrements of the umpiring trade. I bought black steel-toed shoes like those worn by mechanics. The balloon protector I concocted was a homemade facsimile of what I saw the real McCoys use on the field. It was crude and a little rough around the edges, but I was just in the Georgia State League. Maybe they could take a good joke.

Before I actually put on the umpire's suit as an official in the Georgia State League, I never paid much attention to umpires. Like most other players, I considered them to be several steps above a leech gatherer and perhaps a step or two below a carnival barker. They were necessary evils because no one had yet devised an alternative way to make the calls of the game.

My first game as an umpire took place in Sparta, Georgia. It was nice to still be with the guys I was accustomed to seeing on the diamond, but somewhat embarrassing to see them from my vantage point as an umpire. There was a modest thrill in throwing guys out and calling strikes. One player I sent back to the bench trailing his bat and mumbling to himself said, "You couldn't get me out when you were pitching."

I gave him the thumb to the dugout. "Oh yeah, well I can get you out now." I liked the feeling of being the autocrat of the baseball diamond. It opened up whole new vistas of bossing guys around. At least in 1948, my future as a professional umpire seemed as if it could be endurable pleasure, endlessly prolonged. I'd have to put up with college in the meantime, but during summers I'd still be able to umpire in order to keep my hamsters in the style they had grown accustomed to.

Umpires come in all shapes and sizes and from virtually all walks of life. All sorts of people with all sorts of bizarre reasons have decided to make the fateful decision to wear a blue suit. Many, like me, scrambled to get behind the plate because they were ejected from other vocations. I have yet to meet an optometrist who decided to make the big move to baseball officiating. But coal miners, former college officials, ex-teachers, maître d's, ex-football players, insurance men, and even former professional baseball players have ended up on the wrong side of the dugouts. Many of my colleagues in the National League had brighter days in the stadiums as players. Frank Secory once played for the Chicago Cubs, Kenny Burkhart was with the St. Louis Cardinals, Lon Warnecke pitched for the Cards and Cubs, and the great Jocko Conlon once stalked Comiskey Park with the White Sox.

Actually it seems that umpires just became umpires. Any kid who tells his parents he wants to be a professional umpire could easily run the risk of getting smacked on the spot and sent to bed without supper. More appropriately, things happen to other careers that send men running to the umpire ranks for one reason or another. Young men with fascist tendencies particularly enjoy the role of being able to become a one man judge and jury on the field.

When I wasn't playing baseball, basketball, or tennis for High Point, I spent my summers umpiring. Everything from minor league baseball diamonds to amateur leagues and cow pastures were fertile grounds for earning extra money. An athletic scholarship paid the tuition but never put any money in my pockets. I became the college's unofficial social coordinator to earn extra cash. I rented a cabin in the woods near campus that was transformed into North Carolina's premier party headquarters on weekends. Male students paid a nominal cover charge for the privilege of attendance, women were invited at no cost. I sold hamburgers and hot dogs and my record player accompanied their dining and dancing.

I was a fairly good student at High Point College. I didn't do anything to make Oxford or Harvard nervous, but I graduated in 1952 with a B average in my Social Studies major. Spanish, French, and physical education were my minors. Considering how my studies frequently interrupted my athletics, my grade point average should have been measured by a micrometer.

Tennis was an interesting venture into a different world of sports. I thought that if a guy could call himself Pancho Gonzalez and become famous playing the sport, I figured I'd give it a whirl. It was difficult trying to find a pair of tennis sneakers that could accommodate the extra bone in my left ankle. Because there were no official High Point College shorts to fit a polar bear, I had to find a pair of my own. Most intercollegiate sports at High Point involved playing colleges of a similar enrollment. But with tennis this was not the case. We played colleges and universities of all sizes up and down the Eastern seaboard. For a guy from a mill town like Woonsocket, I did surprisingly well against the tennis-prone Ivy Leaguers.

Despite the fact that I wanted to teach, there were a number of professors at college who had their doubts. They knew I was a kid at heart but supposedly that was not sufficient grounds for the makings of a competent teacher.

There were two types of teaching certificates graduating seniors received at North Carolina in the early Fifties. The coveted A certificate meant that a prospective teacher not only had the classroom credentials to teach but also the student teaching experience. The B certificate meant the student had the necessary education classes but lacked the student teaching experience. Virtually all the state boards of education required an A certification as a hiring criteria. Only a few school systems would accept a B certificate and virtually any acceptance to teach hinged on the premise that additional courses would be taken to reach the A level.

Ruth Steelman was High Point's director of practice teaching. She was convinced I was too busy with sports to pay much attention to the academic preparations for teaching. She refused to let me into the all-important practice teaching program. I was irate with her decision. I had a B average and was denied into her coveted domain. This meant I would not only have a rough time finding a teaching job after graduation, but when I found one I'd have to teach a year to qualify for and A certificate.

I managed to vent my frustration in a most mature and professional way. Word had circulated around campus that Miss Steelman was going to Europe for the summer. I waited until my diploma was firmly in my hands when I walked up to her graduation ceremonies. "I heard you are going to Europe this summer," I said.

She told me she was looking forward to the expedition. "Well, I hope the boat sinks," I told her plainly.

One of my most memorable experiences professional baseball was playing for the House of David team in 1952 during my senior year at High Point. Young people who have never heard of this great barnstorming team are apt to think I chased balls for a rabbinical institute. The team was originally organized in Michigan and was rostered with the number of players from that state, but they managed to acquire baseball bums throughout their whirlwind itineraries.

In the truest sense of the barnstorming tradition, the House of David were a bunch of nomads. There was no field, no home town fans. Evidentially, one of the team's original members knew a little about history and modeled the team after the ancient wandering Hebrews. Halting all shaving was not only a team tradition, but a requisite. Without exception, every member of the House of David supported a Moses beard. I joined the team while they were touring North Carolina and as far as the other players were concerned, I must have looked like a clean-shaven Gentile in their line-up. I began pitching without much of a beard. Even as time progressed, my beard growth remained in a kind of remission. I never had much more than a scruffy, spinach chin while my teammates sprouted the Charlton Heston vis-à-vis Mount Sinai look.

The House of David was one of baseball's greatest barnstorming teams and loaded with talent. A number of players not only had years of professional minor league experience, there were some players who had a cup of coffee in majors before being banished forever to the hinterlands of baseball's trampdom.

The team had an excellent reputation and fans flocked to our games around the country. The schedule was a gruesome routine. We would play a game one afternoon in the city, board a single team bus and be prepared to take the field the following afternoon in another city 250 miles away, and be as fresh as a daisy. After a half day of driving on dusty country roads to reach the next town, we invariably looked like a herd of Bedouin tribesmen exiting a bus.

Besides the rough routine of trying to always win on the road, the House of David had a host of skits and comedy routines for the fans. It was part and parcel of the team's tradition. So instead of just barnstorming and playing decent baseball, I had to learn the fundamentals of comedic acting. This was not all that difficult because I'd been accustomed to doing this throughout my minor-league career. Three guys, for instance, would sit on the pitcher's mound and pretend they were fishing in a rowboat. All of us would go through the motions of rowing in tandem. One guy pointed to the sky and follow the flight of a welcomed seabird. When it was over us, it would crap. The bird plucky hit one man in the eye and sent the other two valiant seamen overboard.

Shadow playing was another major part of our theatrical routine. If we played baseball the same way we were capable of shadow playing, the' 49 Yankees wouldn't of stood a prayer. Pitchers threw to catchers without a ball, batters had no balls, outfielders made dashing, imaginary catches while infielders applied their skills in double plays and fantastic fielding maneuvers. All the mannerisms and gyrations of actually using a ball were mimicked to the finest detail.

After graduation from High Point, I accepted a manager's job in Canada's Laurentian League, I had just about recovered from playing with the Lost Tribes the previous year when I signed to manage a tough group of off-season hockey players who spoke French. I was an incorrigible glutton for all the bizarre that baseball had to offer.

The Laurentian League was comprised of semi-pro teams around Montréal. I managed a team from St. George de Beauce in the rolling countryside north of the city. Hockey was still king amongst these athletes. Baseball was regarded as a nice way to stay in shape when the ice was too thin to skate. League rules permitted a maximum of four non-Canadians on any Laurentian squad. I took full advantage of this and invited four friends from North Carolina to join me because I needed someone on the field to remind the Canadians that body slams and board checks are not stylish in baseball.

English was an exotic foreign language to most of the Canadian players. This was no real problem, however, because my four friends from the U.S. felt the same way. I grew up in Woonsocket and knew French since I was in short pants. Most of the town was comprised of French-Canadians who had ventured south of the border to work in the mills. French and Spanish were also my academic minors at High Point College, so I at least felt adequate in communicating with the players. This understanding of the language came in handy because it made me adept in picking up some of the dangling participles my players and other managers recited that never seem to be included in the classier textbooks of the time.

An honest week's schedule included five night games and a Sunday afternoon match. Because the league consisted of teams in and around the general Montréal area, travel was not an ordeal. We played other squads in the league with such Continental names as LaChute, Lachine, St. Jerome, and Chateauiguay.

A first look at my team made me realize I was not managing a squad of intellectuals. Most of the guys looked like they had been models for dental school textbooks. Years of hockey had creatively restricted their teeth and noses. Gaps in their ivories told the painful tales of past games when pucks had careened off their jaws.

While they were hockey players first and baseball was further down their list of priorities, they were still good athletes. Once they realized a bat had to be dropped when a hit was made instead of being used to knock a player on the field off a base, we began to speak the same language.

My wife, Carleen, and I were married that season in St. George de Beauce, Québec. We had met as college students at High Point. Although she was a North Carolinian and I was a misplaced Yankee, my managing that season precluded me from leaving the team and traveling to North Carolina. Carleen joined me north of the border and we were married on August 1, 1952. It seemed so romantic to be joined in marriage in a region of a foreign country that spoke another language. Besides the French-speaking dental anomalies, the Royal Canadian Mounted Police were also at my wedding. I think the Canadians understood enough about baseball to realize that the RCMP's were a good idea. A manager's wedding, like umpires, should be policed to avoid the throwing of anything but rice and bouquets. Home

CHAPTER THREE

JUST A MINOR AFFAIR

"Being in position to see the play is the main thing, you must never leave a base or play unguarded." –Paul Pryor

After World War II, everyone who could throw overhand wanted to play professional baseball. Any burg, hamlet, village, or township large enough to host a gathering of any kind seem to have a minor league team. Thousands of young players high on hopes were funneled into the vast network of minor circuits that crisscrossed the country.

The eventual demise of this great system in the succeeding decades was not attributable to the players' loss of inspiration or desire to play someday besides their heroes in the majors. The gradual urbanization of the nation brought people closer to cities with big league teams. Television was the most instrumental device in shutting many minor league parks for good. Fans that normally would see their local minor league club play on a Monday or Thursday night could turn on the TV in their living rooms and see the big leaguers. While the Atwater Kent radios and a weekly, monthly, or seasonal trip to the local ballpark once satisfied fans' interests, television changed the old local parks forever. Why listen to a game on the radio or visit a Single-A minor league park when the guy from Dubuque could watch Ernie Lombardi of the Reds or Stan Musial of the Cards in living black and white? Baseball fans did not so much turn down tickets to the local minor league games as they turned on the television and watch the big leaguers under new TV screens. It was a greater thrill to see Bobby Feller throw a shutout on TV than it was to envision him from the radio or watch Joe Palooka on the team down the road pitch to a roster of no-name players. It was just that simple.

Despite the fact that the minor league systems today are only a fraction of their early post-war size, their purpose remains unchanged. They are still the school of fundamentals, the weeding ground, and experimental center for professional players. But the reduced size of the minors has recently led baseball to turn toward the college ranks are bright young prospects.

Colleges are becoming more competitive in recruiting talented players from the ranks of high school squads. Junior colleges and four-year institutions in the Belt States of the South, the Southwest, and California have longer playing seasons than their northern competitors. Many players in these areas participate in their colleges' training and playing schedules as well as join winter league teams.

But very few collegiate stars automatically make that quantum leap to the majors. Colleges are fertile grounds for selecting talented players for the minor leagues, but they cannot be considered substitutes for the minors.

A healthy college schedule may involve 30 or 40 games a season. Minor league clubs today play about 120-130 games a year. After one year on a minor league team, a player is bound to be more experienced than his collegiate counterpart. This experience is not simply attributed to the additional number of games played, but includes a more varied range of pitchers and pitching styles, and opportunities for base stealing.

In 1953, I left umpiring to manage the Pierre Cowboys in the Basin League. I discovered the hard way just how difficult it was for college grads to cope with the minors. The league was comprised totally of NCAA athletes. Most were standouts on their college teams and serious enough about the sport to spend their entire summer vacations on the sun-based, unwashed planes of the upper Midwest playing baseball.

A pre-season glance at my team's roster gave me outrageous hopes. I was convinced I had a squad of future Hall-of-Famers who are going to shatter every hitting record and every other team in the Basin League. But I soon watched the guys with collegiate averages of .390 and .410 fall to a paltry .220 or .225. Most of the players on my team had never faced a varied selection of pitchers. I discovered many with slugger averages in competitive college conferences had never faced a good curveball pitcher before. Some .350 hitters had only rarely seen a burning fastball. Many were accustomed to the sluggish two or three games per week schedules and wilted in the midst of a four and five game playing week.

Technically, while the minors are not the best training and staging grounds for young players, on a human level it can be a purgatory for those baseball souls vanquished from the majors. After a few months in the minor circuits, a player or umpire comes to require a completely different state of mind.

41

Everything from salaries to stadiums are a shoddier facsimile of life in the big leagues. National and American League parks have umpires' locker rooms with carpets, color TVs, refrigerators, and showers with 20th century plumbing. Minor league parks have dressing rooms for umpires too, but they look like the solitary confinement cells at Devil's Island. While one guy showers beneath a single, rusty spicket on a stained cement floor, his partner waits for his turn on the only other available seat – the john. The majors schedule gala events like T-Shirt Day or the admission of a former player into the Hall of Fame with a pre-game ceremony. The minor leagues have beer nights. Although they may attract more people than the country fair, a bunch of beered-up Bolsheviks in a rickety park with virtually no security is like a bomb ready to explode.

While I was learning about life in the minors during springs and summers, I was pulling my crew cut out by the roots in the classroom. Teaching seemed like an ideal avocation to accompany my umpiring. I enjoyed being with children and accepted my daily work as a challenge. Like umpiring, no day was ever the carbon copy of another. If I could dismiss my last class and realized I had imparted my students with more knowledge than when they walked into that classroom, I had accomplished no small victory.

The U.S. Navy refused to rent me a small cruiser to strafe Miss Steelman's European-bound ship, so I taught in Gibson, North Carolina, for a year and qualified for my A certificate. In 1953, I taught high school and Middlebury and joined the Carolina League as an umpire. Besides teaching during the school season, I coached basketball and baseball. As a teacher-umpire in Littleton, North Carolina I officiated the state championship and made home plate calls for Gaylord and Jim Perry. I knew these guys were going to be stars someday. In the course of the seven inning high school game, they were averaging 17-18 strikeouts.

Throughout most of the Fifties, I rambled about my little corner of the South teaching school and following the Carolina League and Southern Athletic League shuffle during the summers. I taught high school social studies in Williamston and became principal of the high school in Weldon before moving on to metropolitan Bethel Hill in Gibsonville. I even managed to teach chemistry in high school without blowing myself up in the lab. I never got the opportunity to reach Mayberry, so Opey Taylor was never enrolled in any of my classes.

I discovered early in my minor league umpiring career that driving to ballparks was a hazardous ordeal. Major league travel schedules and the more complicated logistics of shuffling from one city to another with four man crews virtually precludes the idea of driving to the stadium. It is more efficient and less troublesome to taxi from the airport to the park and then to the hotel afterwards. In the majors, if we were lucky, sometimes a clubhouse man would pick us up at the airport and whisk the crew directly to the ballpark. This was not only the most efficient means of getting to and from the stadium, but it alleviated some of the post-game rituals minor league fans perform around an umpire's car.

Umpiring in the minors is not simply traveling to a small or mid-sized city to officiate a game. In the lower ranks of the minor league strata, and umpire travels to the fans' neighborhood to work. The ballparks are smaller, a few thousand or even several hundred fans pass through the turnstiles. The parking lots are less spacious and an umpire's car sticks out like a giant target.

An unpopular call on one of the home team's players can inspire some of the local budding Picassos and Rembrandts to express their artistic inspirations on an umpire's car. Toilet paper, soap, enamel and spray paint are just some of the varied artistic mediums used by fans to enhance the car's original Detroit artwork. Sometimes fans will experiment in the junk sculpture genre by displaying an umpire's car on the rustic, cinderblock kind of pedestal.

I made a very unpopular call in 1948 during my first year as an umpire in the Georgia State League. The hometown fans of Fitzgerald, Georgia, became slightly rebellious at my decision on the field and different conspiracies were plotted throughout the stands. I had visions of making the big time that night. I thought I'd end up on the front page of the Atlanta *Constitution's* sport's page – "Rhode Island Yankee Lynched by the Peach State's Good Ole Boys" – complete with a full page of photos.

I walked to my car in the parking lot after the game, started the engine and thought I had somehow eluded the angry masses when I discovered my car wouldn't budge. The engine roared and the wheels turn, but my car stood still in the warm Georgia night. I got out and discovered that Coca-Cola crates were strategically placed under the axles so that the wheels were just a fraction of an inch off the pavement. The town sheriff had about as much sympathy for me as Torquemada did for a heathen during the Spanish Inquisition. Evidently, *everyone* in Fitzgerald was a baseball fan and the town Constable was no exception. If it wasn't for the fact he was called to my disabled car on official business, I'm sure he would have been the ringleader of the necktie party. As soon as my car was off the crates, he agreed to escort me to the edge of town. After that, I would have to fend for myself. Under his watchful eye, I raced to the Fitzgerald border. But to add insult to injury, after only three miles on the road my car coughed, choked, sputtered, and then suffered a fatal case of food poisoning. Dirt had been poured in my gas tank while parked and it took just a few miles of driving for the Georgia red clay to work its way into the engine.

Schooling has become a necessary credential for virtually every umpire aspiring to enter the ranks of professional baseball. The days of barnstorming umpires like me reaching the minor leagues, let alone the majors, by putting in their time on the way up the hawse pipe are over. What's Sputnik did to change American education – big money players, TV rights, free agency, and the growing complexities of the game have changed the credentials of umpires forever.

The Joe Brinkman and Harry Wendelstedt Umpiring Schools attract not only the guys that want a career in the pros, but sports enthusiasts and laymen who want to thoroughly know the rules of baseball. Graduation from either school is bound to make someone a better umpire whether he is planning to officiate high school games or enter the professional ranks. Both schools give a complete course in the mechanics and fundamentals of the sport. Nearly every play in the rulebook is gone over and over again. They learn the right way to call balls and strikes, where to position themselves for better calling, and finish knowing the rulebook better than Moses knew the Bible.

Applying the theoretical knowledge of umpires' school to the minors is usually difficult. What works on the instructional diamonds in Florida is not always the case in the majors. Minor league umpires have to be more emphatic than their colleagues in the majors. A clear call and a raised arm is sufficient to indicate a strike in the big leagues. In my untutored way, I raised my fists like Jack Dempsey for a strike behind the plate. Some umpires performed a flying camel with the double axel and then pirouetted softly to the turf. But a raised arm is essentially a standard indicator of a strike. This simple maneuver is not easily understood in the minor league ranks. Many younger players there are exposed to professional umpires for the first time. They are more accustomed to straining in order to decipher the hodge-podge of calls and gyrations made by high school and amateur league umpires.

The most important thought in physically making a call is to be emphatic. Players must understand the umpire's decision on a call. As in the majors, the minor league umpire may raise an arm and bellow, bark, or howl a strike call. Once someone puts on the blue umpire's suit, the whole world treats you like an oyster. Even your own father-in-law begins to dislike you. Friendships are lost at the drop of an asinine call. Prospective umpires are made aware of this at the two schools, but it takes a baptism in the minor league fires for the point to be branded into their hides as fact. Professional umpires rant and rave on the school fields to simulate a berserk manager for their students, but that's still playing for the special effects. It's not until the real thing in the minors charges out of the dugout with veins popping, tobacco spraying, and chanting ugly participles that makes a young umpire a true believer.

A friend can easily become your enemy as soon as you wear the blue suit. I once drove to High Point with a friend where I was umpiring a Carolina League game between the HiToms and the Durham Bulls. I knew my pal was a Durham fan, but it hardly seemed important to our friendship. Around the seventh inning, I made a call that caused some of the Durham supporters to pull their hair out by the roots in frustration. The fan that screamed the loudest for my blood was my friend in the stands. I couldn't believe it. This was the unkindest cut of all. I walked over to the stands where he was seated and asked, "By the way, how are you getting home tonight, anyways?"

In many ways, umpiring in the minors is much more frustrating than in the big leagues. The stands are usually closer to the diamonds for one thing. The term "stadium security" is virtually nonexistent in the minor-league lexicon. A dubious call on a hometown player can cause plans to tear down the rafters and then chase you with them. Sometimes the entire stands will chant jeers a cappella at umpires.

Any game at Macon, Georgia's ballpark is always a treacherous event. Players, fans, and umpires are kept busy in the humid nights doing battle with the squadrons of mosquitoes that look like small F-16 fighters. Beside the small stadium is a train depot. The rumbling of incoming and outgoing trains in the adjacent yards nicely lends some realistic sound effects to the mosquito bombardments.

It was frequently my misfortune to make a call that the Macon fans dislike just when the train was chugging away from the depot. There were all sorts of suggestions as to where I could go on the departing train. After some disagreeable calls, choruses of "Put Pryor on that train! Hey, someone put Pryor on that train and get him the hell out of here!" was a frequent travel suggestion.

One of the most frustrating things for a player or umpire is to realize that the minors may be the peak and end of his professional career. I've been down that road a few hundred times myself. The glory and glitter of pro baseball belongs to the majors. The greasy diners, endless bus rides to nowhere, and the horrible hot dogs in dilapidated parks frequently accompany minor league ball.

Outstanding minor league players and umpires do not always find their way up to the majors. Besides the detectable skills and talents that separate an excellent from the good or adequate players, Lady Luck has much to say about an athlete becoming a big leaguer. Each rookie player or umpire in the majors thinks back from time to time on the great minor league men left behind. Even after 20 years in the majors, I can remember umpires in the American Association who were as good as any umpire anywhere, anytime in the big parks.

I umpired with Dave Carraba for one year in the American Association before being called by the National League. I always thought it was a shame Dave never got the chance to break into the majors. He is one of the best umpires I've ever worked with. When the Palace of Perseverance is built beside the Hall of Fame in Cooperstown, New York, Dave is entitled to a life -sized bronze statue.

Free agency is a grand imperial kudos enjoyed by major league players. But outstanding minor league players have more of a realistic need for the whole free agency concept than their big league counterparts. A catcher trapped behind Johnny Bench in Cincinnati's minor system could have a great arm, a .400 errorless season with 35 homeruns and still remain in the minors for years. Any first baseman behind Ernie Banks on the Cubs' farm team could have the best composite minor league record for the season, but watch helplessly as other players on the team are elevated to the majors. Some minor leaguers are caught in a great player's shadow and lived there for years. After seeing situations like this, I've come to realize that free agency should not be just for the men in the majors. The big leaguers already enjoy outrageous salaries. Free agency permits them to have an extra helping of the icing. The players trapped behind a Berra or Mantle, who are good enough to have a shot at the majors should at least be given an opportunity without having to wait for a retirement. It's an unnecessary waste of talent and short circuits the flow of qualified minor league players into the majors.

The bush leagues have a number of unique players who, for one reason or another, have tremendously lopsided talents and credentials. Some guys are fantastic hitters, but couldn't catch a measly pop-up to save their minor league souls. Major league scouts look at these characters and report back to their organizations with the notations – OFFENSE – could be another Hank Aaron, a great hitter – DEFENSE – forget it, guys! Players with such unbalanced qualities are rarely called up to the big leagues. The advent of the American League's designated hitter may be their only saving grace.

Willie Duke played for the Durham Bulls in the Carolina League. His talents were so one-sided that he tipped the scales of the imagination. Of all my years as a player and umpire, rarely have I ever seen a better hitter. Not only was he always a long-ball threat, but he could strategically place a ball with relative ease. But Willie's problem was that he had absolutely no ability as a defenseman. A lazy, trailing ball on the ground or an easy pop fly were unbelievably difficult for him to handle. He might have well have fielded balls catapulted from the top of castle walls. Balls hit him, they bounced off his body, they tipped off his glove, even hit him in the head. Apparently he was so geared to only hit that no one bothered to tell him baseballs had to be caught in the outfield, not stopped by his body and then retrieved.

While the minors may be the poor sister to the majors, they are rich in characters. Per square stadium, there are more jokers in the farm systems than in virtually any other part of the baseball world. Their rosters abound with nuts, kooks, schizophrenics, crazies, practical jokers as well as the common garden variety, comical and criminally insane and inane, and guys who are just funny in spite of themselves. Not only have the bizarre of the majors passed through the minors, but bush league tramps with loose screws are commonplace. For this reason, umpires don't have to feel lonely in the minors. Although people have always thought umps operated on less then all cylinders, there are a lot of players, coaches, and especially managers in the same strange state of mind. But while nutty players and managers with talent are still raised to the majors, many crazy umpires are prohibited from big league ball. I never thought this was fair.

"Turkey" Tyson was one of the most memorable characters to ever play the National Pastime. He was a first baseman with the Durham Bulls during the time I was an umpire with the Carolina

League and one of the wackiest people who ever learned to throw overhand.

"Turkey" had a high-pitched voice and could become so excited in the field that he actually gobbled. He would encourage his team's pitcher by yelling "Come on, get him out! Get them out! Come on, get him out! Get him out!" From the stands he sounded like a prize tom turkey. The closer the game, the more he would encourage his pitcher. During the ninth inning of a tied game, his gobbles became so frequent that it seemed as though a poultry farm had been let loose on the field.

One (believe it or not) great umpire in the Carolina League had a terrible pet peeve about pitchers who doctored the ball. I purposefully withhold his name to protect the guilty. For the record, I'll call him A.T.

I was a member of A.T.'s crew for one game in the 1950's when the league's most notorious spitballer was scheduled to start a game. This guy had more of a reputation for throwing a doctored ball that he did for orchestrating a good game. Everyone in the Carolina League knew he threw a phony ball, but he was a coy operator. As umpires' luck would have it, however, we never managed to examine just the *right* ball. Some of his pitches performed enough gravity defying maneuvers in the air to make Sir Isaac Newton roll over in his grave. When he couldn't legitimately send the batter to the dugout kicking his heels, he'd send him back with goofball pitches.

Home plate umpires in the minors will usually prepare between 2 ½-3 dozen balls for a game. Depending upon the conditions of the field, major league umpires will ready 5-6 dozen or more balls in preparation for a game.

A.T. had the home plate assignment for the Carolina League's ace spitball pitcher. As he began to take the shine off the balls, a playful glint came to his eyes. I knew something was afoot, but it wasn't until he finished rubbing down the balls when I realized the extent of his temporary insanity.

A.T. was convinced that if this pitcher could screw-up the game undetected, then he could screw-up the pitcher undetected. After he finished warming-up the balls, he proceeded to amass all three dozen of them on the shower floor of the umpires' dressing room. I thought this was the convenient new way of ridding the balls of their lacquer-like finish until he started to urinate on them. And urinate he did! Everything escaped him.

Afterwards, he methodically went through the process of sanding all three dozen to remove any traces of moisture. It took a few innings before the pitcher started to get in trouble on the mound. Around the sixth inning, almost like clockwork, he began to lick his fingers. A.T. wasn't going to inspect *any* balls that night.

The pitcher threw doctored balls for most of the latter innings and won the game 4-3. A.T. didn't particularly care if the guy won or lost when he was behind the plate, he just enjoyed watching him lick his fingers.

In the umpires' locker room after the game, A.T. had a slight change of heart about the escapade. He wasn't as proud about pulling off such an outrageous stunt as he was about the good luck he claimed to have brought the pitcher. Now he seemed glad the spitballer won. He strutted around the showers, pleased as punch out his new-found charm. "He won because of my urination," he boasted. From the way he talked, the rest of us were convinced he was considering entering the bottling business on the side.

Minor league managers are hilarious to watch when they become cranky. Steam billows from their ears, their eyes cross, their blood pressure tops a battleship's boiler and they scream harsh metaphors. This is basically the same reaction as their counterparts in the majors, but with one important difference. There is a sense, (although a small one), of restraint in the majors. Managers there are aware of the more thorough and ever-present press corps. Their infractions and misconduct on the field will be retold in all the gory details by the electronic and print media. They also realize that their transgressions will be witnessed by thousands of fans and a big league stadium. Certainly the Durochers, Weavers, and Martins of the baseball world will continue their forays, but they are more the exceptions than the rule. The minor league manager is not handicapped by these major league restraints. An irate manager in the bush leagues is capable of anything when he is incensed.

I knew a number of major league umpires when they were still bus jockeys in the farm systems. In the big leagues, they acted like normal, mature managers – they swore like Marine drill sergeants, kicked dirt, and danced around in utter frustration. When they were in the minors, however, they climbed flagpoles, dug holes in the infield dirt, stole bases from the diamonds, jumped over the outfield walls. The minor league managerial ethos is simple – just don't get mad at the umpires, get even!

One night in 1957, I was scheduled to work base duty in a game between the High Point and Durham clubs. My wife dropped me off at the High Point field and drove to the movie theater to watch the early evening show. Because I had a field assignment that night, I decided to leave my balloon protector and home plate equipment the car.

My pal, Junius Beck, was slated to call balls and strikes that night. But early in the game, Junius was hit behind the plate and had to leave the field. Before he made his untimely trip to the showers, he was good enough to bequeath me his inside protector. I wasn't accustomed to the inside chest pad at this point in my career, but I put on Junius' contraption, hoped for the best, and moved behind the plate to complete the game.

The great Chicago Cubs' manager, Charlie Metro, was then the skipper of the Durham Bulls. Charlie was my nemesis during my days with the Carolina League. We were slightly less compatible on the field that Saint Patrick and a boa constrictor. No call could suit Charlie's liking and he was not above registering his opinion from the dugout. In 1957, I had to run Charlie off the field seven times. For an umpire with a relatively high tolerance threshold for irate managers, that was a harvest season.

During the fifth inning of the game, I was hit by a ball that almost flattened my Adam's apple. Charlie thought this was just great. While I was holding my neck in agony, he shouted loud and clear, "It should have killed you!"

My patience had been wearing thin with him all night but the lousy display of his bedroom manner was the final straw. After I threw him out of the game, he made another wisecrack just as a second helping to really infuriate me.

Charlie knew that during the off-season I was a teacher in a high school basketball coach. While he should have been thinking about a clean towel and a full bar of soap on his way to the showers, he turned around and shouted, "I hope you lose every game this season!"

Charlie hated umpires even more than the average red blooded baseball fan. If he had his run of the game, he would manage his team and make all the umpiring calls directly from the dugout. Even before the first pitch was thrown or the first swing taken by a batter, Charlie began to ride the umpires.

On one memorable occasion, I threw him out of the park before the game even started. I had the plate assignment for a Durham game when both managers approached me with their line-up cards. Charlie made the motions of presenting his team's roster, but just before I was able to take it, he let it drop. The card fluttered helplessly in the air like a feather while Charlie made no effort to retrieve it.

"If that card lands on home plate, you're out of the game," I told him as all three of us watch the line-up card slowly sail to earth. True to Newton's Laws, the card finally landed right on the plate and Charlie was in the showers lathering his back before the first pitch was thrown.

The minor league managers' spirit of getting both mad and even with an umpire can be carried to some strange lengths. Sometimes crazed managers will perform a stunt on the field that is supposed to infuriate an umpire. Most of the time, this psychology falls far short of its intended designs. I liked it when they did something outrageous – so did the fans. Many times when I was supposed to be furious with rage, I stood on the field laughing at them.

Frank Lucchesi managed at High Point in the Carolina League during the late Fifties. Following his tour of duty in the minors, he managed the Philadelphia Phillies, the Texas Rangers, and works as a scout in the Dodgers' organization.

Frank was a thorough student of baseball and a very competent team skipper, but he was another member of that dubious school of managers who felt they were entitled to naturally assume the dual roles of manager and umpire. He frequently resented the fact that baseball had given umpires the responsibility of making calls on the field. That was the big shortcoming of Abner Doubleday's whole plan.

Frank was extremely high strung in the dugout. Many times the bench would vibrate from his nervous gyrations. Once in High Point, I made a call that Frank disagreed with so much that out of sheer frustration he ran out to center field and climbed the flagpole in protest. He didn't get all the way up and we didn't have to call the fire department to get down, but it was funny to watch him shimmy like a little bear.

Frank Skaff was another minor league manager who could send umpires to the Home for the Definitely Neurotic long before their time. I had the home plate assignment one night in Winston-Salem when the Cardinals were hosting his Durham club.

Around the fifth inning, I made a call at the plate that Frank objected to. He charged onto the field and read me a litany of licentious cognates. The only way to cool him off was to force him to take an early shower. I gave him a thumb over the shoulder trying to get the game underway again.

The Winston-Salem Stadium is a very unusual structure, to say the very least. The locker room for the visiting team was built more or less as an afterthought. Out-of-town players have to walk all the way down the right field line just to enter the dressing room. Somehow the architect mistook the bullpen for the visiting teams' lockers and installed dressing benches and shower spigots instead of a couple of pitching mounds. Even more interesting is the fact that there is no such thing as a quick getaway for a visiting manager. He is forced to parade past angry stands to the end of the right field line. This does wonders to someone's psychological stability. While the evicted manager is already irate about an umpire's call and then getting the "bums rush" from the umpire – on top of all that, he has to take a long walk to the dressing room in the Carolina night beside fans screaming dangling diphthongs at him.

Frank Skaff also had a unique style of walking. He was powerfully pigeon-toed and, as a consequence, from the back view, he appeared to waddle. Frank's baggy uniform pants, his waddle along the victory lap to the mile-away showers, and the fans threatening to draw and quarter him, all proved hilarious.

As Frank was heading to the visitors' locker room, his 13-year-old son ran out on the field and asked me why I decided to throw his dad out of the game. I explained to the boy my call at home plate and how I couldn't possibly tolerate his father's actions on the field.

The kids listened attentively and then looked up at me and declared, "Well, whatever he said goes for me, too."

"Well, then, you better get ready to wash her father's back," I informed him.

Frank's loyal son took my suggestions seriously and began the long trek after his father. The boy was a chip off the old block, right down to the pigeon-toed feet and waddle. The sight of Frank parading by the right field stands was funny enough, but the appearance of the son waddling in his wake was hilarious.

In 1974, I told this story at a sports banquet in Baltimore. Afterwards, a member of the audience approached me and said he remembered the incident Winston-Salem. Lo and behold, it was Frank Skaff's son, grown and working as an attorney.

I was never a born screamer, but running a team in the Basin League for a season gave me excellent credentials for opening an employment agency or personnel service. All the league's players were NCAA athletes who emigrated from their campuses to play a summer of baseball in the upper Midwest. Because of their amateur status, none of the athletes were paid. They played baseball on a minor league level and attracted minor league size crowds in minor league parks, but because of their NCAA status, no one was entitled to be paid for any sports activities.

Besides the responsibilities of maintaining a competitive team, overseeing practices, arranging transportation and becoming the squad's chaplain, doctor, lawyer, and romance counselor, I also had to find jobs for my team. This is no small task considering the fact that our hometown was bustling Pierre, South Dakota. The team was not overburdened with wheat shockers and cornhuskers. Many players were even under the impression that the Dakotas were small European countries located somewhere between Poland and Czechoslovakia.

Fortunately, the people of the state's capital city were supportive of their team. Many merchants who hired summer help were willing to include some players on their payrolls. Painting seem to be a popular summer vocation. I had guys painting and repainting lines on the runways of the Pierre airport. Some unfortunates could be found deep fried under the hot prairie sun painting miles and miles of center strips on roads leading to nowhere. Other budding Renaissance men painted homes around the town.

The Basin League was actually comprised of the nation's best collegiate baseball players at the time. Steve Boros, the former Oakland A's manager and skipper of the San Diego Padres was one of my players on the Pierre Cowboys. No doubt, Steve will readily admit that most of his managing experience came as a result of watching me in the dugout and taking copious notes. I managed against other Basin League teams rostered with players like Ron Perranowski, Frank Howard, Bob Gibson, and Dick Hawser, the former Yankee manager and field boss of the 1985 World Champion Kansas City Royals. The thought that I became their role model and mentor during their formative baseball years has been no small consolation to me in the intervening years.

One crushing bureaucratic decision in the minors nearly made me a permanent spectator of the sport. In 1959, Sam Smith, president of the Southern Athletic League issued a decree that the league would no longer use teachers as umpires. His new Papal Bull was earthshattering for me not only because I wanted to be an umpire, but it was also a vital supplement to my teaching and coaching salaries.

For one reason or another, Sam Smith thought my teaching was a little too taxing for the league's front offices. The most desirable umpires, as far as he was concerned were guys who did absolutely nothing except umpire full-time. These were the characters who didn't have to get up until noon every day and then hung out in poolrooms until game time. This seemed preferable to an umpire who worked another job. Presumably, the day's occupation would mentally distract an umpire at night or he may be waylaid during his day's work and not be able to make game time. The league officially announced that they wanted umpires dedicated enough to want to make it all the way to the major leagues. Teaching was deemed to be mentally distracting and they wanted to keep clear-minded, prospective big leaguers off this designated course.

Umpiring in the Class-A SALLY League was actually a huge leap from the lowly Class B Carolina League. Besides working a higher class of baseball, I was resurrected from Greensboro and High Point to some of the exciting mid-sized cities like Asheville, Charlotte, Columbia, Knoxville, Jacksonville, Macon, Savannah, and Columbus. The pay was better and the per diem allowance was a tad more reasonable, but now all that seemed down the tubes with Sam Smith's untimely decision.

Not long after my banishment from pro baseball, Smith called me in North Carolina and asked if I was available to work two games in Asheville. Russ Goetz, another SALLY League umpire who later became a great American League umpire, had just been married but before the honeymoon was over Russ and his new bride developed some marital problems. Sam told me Goetz needed some time by himself to sort out his problems and asked if I could cover a couple of Russ's games. This is like receiving a pardon from Hades.

I worked the two day Asheville stint and by the end of the week, Sam called me again. Evidently he came to the conclusion that teachers were far more reliable than he ever anticipated. I was supposed to be the guy who couldn't work certain games because the school lab blew up or because I had to stay late with a couple kids on detention.

Sam rescinded his teacher band on the phone and wanted to rehire me. I had the crazy idea of trying my hand at labor negotiations on the phone with him. I hemmed and hawed and played hard to get, but in the end it worked. Before I hung up the receiver, Sam had rehired me as a SALLY League umpire with a salary increase. I got everything I wanted and more while Sam was ready for his bed at baseball's Home for Lobotomy Candidates.

By the end of the 1960 season, I had a severe relapse of the baseball blahs. Moving from city to city in the SALLY League was getting old fast. I was still driving around the South in a Class-A league dreaming of the promise land in Yankee Stadium or Wrigley Field. Even if I was promoted to a triple-A league, there was still the chance I'd remain there for another geological epoch before moving to the majors. Worst of all, I could become a nameless baseball statistic – another umpire who grew old and tired in the minors without ever reaching the big parks.

Just when I started to take some long, hard looks at myself in the morning mirror, I was granted a reprieve from another SALLY League season. The triple-A American Association purchased my contract for the '61 season. At least now I'd be a heartbeat and a phone call away from the majors. I was hired at a whopping $5500 a year salary and would travel by plane from one game to another. Instead of Macon and Savannah, I'd get to see the bright lights of Louisville, Indianapolis, and Houston.

Near the end of my rookie season with the American Association, I discovered that the Great Commissioner in the sky was looking out for me after all. On September 8, 1961, Fred Fleig, the national League's supervisor of umpires, called me at the Kentucky Hotel in Louisville. "Are you the guy they called the Carolina Teacher?"

I had an instant case of the Jimmy Stewart humdiddy, humdiddy, humdiddies before I said, "Yeah, I guess that's what they call me."

Fred Fleig called to say that my triple-A contract had just been purchased by the National League for $5000. I was officially made a big leaguer in one quick phone call.

Actually the National League's decision to take me on as a rookie was more than a shock. I'd been scouted by officials from both major leagues, and word has circulated that American League President Joe Cronin was ready to promote me to the majors. My contract was drawn-up and collecting dust on his desk. The only thing it lacked was his signature, and until his name and mine were on the dotted line, it was still only a dream. *The Sporting News* carried a small piece claiming that Lee Weyer, Frank Walsh, and I had just joined the National League. No one bothered to tell me. The article was printed and circulated by the News, but no one had officially contacted me until I receive Fleig's notice.

The phone call made my rise to the National League effective immediately. I would have joined the majors within a day or two after Fleig's notification, but problems arose among some of the other American Association umpires.

I was originally scheduled to umpire the play-offs between Indianapolis and Houston. But instead of joining the majors on September 10th or 11th as planned, some of my triple-A colleagues insisted that the new big league umpire should work the Association series with them. I was dying to be in Dodger Stadium or the Polo Grounds instead of Indianapolis, but I understood the feelings of the Association umpires so I arranged plans to join the National League as soon as the play-offs were over. I itched to be behind a major league plate, but I wasn't going to abandon my friends and colleagues without properly finishing my rookie season with them.

After the final game in Indianapolis, I brought the crew out to celebrate. St. Elmo's was one of the finest steakhouses in the Midwest and a popular spot for American Association umpires in Indianapolis. Izzy, the owner, was a good friend to umpires who came in and stumbled out his doors. I decided that since I was now a big league umpire, I'd treat the crew in a big league way. We celebrated over thick steaks and round after round of cold beer. Izzy told me afterwards that he had never seen a man drink as much beer as I did that night.

Fleig contacted me again to mention that my first National League game would be on September 16, in Philadelphia. The first thing I did after hanging-up the receiver was buy a decent suitcase. I took off for Philadelphia from the Charlotte, North Carolina airport. As I walked up the stairway to the plane to wave goodbye to my family and well-wishers, my suitcase broke and my clothes flew all over the runway. This was a real class act from a fledging big leaguer. I think the incident became something of a subliminal suggestion for me. When I decided to begin my sports luggage business, I found that the memories of my BVD's being blown down the runway made a permanent impression on my mind. Home

CHAPTER FOUR

DIFFERENCES BETWEEN MAJORS AND MINORS

"I went from a tiny crossroads town to the major leagues in one year...All I have to do to keep my job is hustle and keep my nose clean. Be on time. Stay on message. Answer the bell" -Paul Pryor

The differences between the minors and the majors are as great as the disparity between Beacon Hill and Mount Everest. The tablecloths at restaurants in big league cities seem brighter, flight accommodations are first class instead of the minor seats next to the commode. The pay is better and the greenbacks always seemed greener.

During my year with the American Association, umpires were allotted $8.33 per diem expenses. This hardly covered the laundry, meals, tips, taxis to and from the airport and stadium, and the sundry expenses of living on the road. My top salary and triple-A baseball was $550 a month, barely enough to keep me, my family, and my hamsters in the lifestyle we had become accustomed to. The $6500 a season major league salary and the $28 per diem allotment made me feel more like a baseball owner than an umpire.

Besides the big league accoutrements of pay, hotels, air flights, the single greatest difference between the minors and majors, for an umpire, is the stadiums. The vastness of the parks is striking. A new big leaguer feels lonesome and small in the expanse of the field and stands. The new parks of the early Sixties like Shea, Candlestick, Busch, Dodger Stadium, Riverfront, Three Rivers, and the Astrodome put the rickety old minor fields of clapboard to shame.

On a first trip to the umpires' locker room, the rookie has to pinch himself and ask if it's real or just a dream. Gone are the paltry days of Neanderthal plumbing in rusty, dilapidated shower rooms. The minor league philosophy was – what the heck? – umpires can dress and shower anywhere. In the majors, toilets magically flush and carpeting replaces damp cement floors. No longer does an umpire have to use the john for a seat while his partner showers in a facility built for a gulags barracks. More than three umpires can maneuver freely without bumping into one another. There is an unusual and exciting feeling in a major league dressing rooms that someone, somewhere, really does think umpires are human beings too!

But even with the advent of the new stadium building in the early Sixties, umpires were given a low priority on the architects' drawing tables. The Astrodome was a big, beautiful, new park with luxurious seats, controlled temperatures and an umpires' dressing room that was as big as a modest water closet when it was built. Shortly after the ribbon-cutting ceremonies, the Astrodome's management acceded to the umpires' demands that their locker room be built a little more spacious. Walls were knocked down and a new dressing was equipped with chairs, a couch, a refrigerator and a color television.

I was fortunate to have been called to the majors in 1961 when several of the old National League ballparks were still in business. These were the history-laden stadiums brought to life over the Atwater Kent radio in my grandparents' home. Because the stands in so many of the older parks were close to the diamond, an umpire or player could easily walk down the first or third base lines and talk to the fans. Fans along the first base line in Pittsburgh's Forbes Field had great seats. Game after game they sat in the same seas. I used to walk the first base line and chat with the same Forbes faithful in the same seats, game after game.

The biggest problem with the old parks was the tough ground rules. You had to have a Ph.D. from M.I.T. to fully understand them. Until an umpire actually put in the necessary time in the old parks, deciphering all the stadiums' strange nuances and odd ground rules was like understanding Tibetan trigonometry.

Connie Mack Stadium in Philadelphia was built around overhangs. Every place in the park seemed to have an overhang jutting out. Consequently, there were more ground rules in that stadium than the Pope had blessings on Easter Sunday. Crosley Field was encumbered by all sorts of markers. A hit to the right of a certain line connoted a home run, one to the left of that same line translated into a double. Wrigley Field was an umpire's complete nightmare until the outfield trough was constructed. Fans would reach over the wall and grab the ball. While the trough prevented much of the fans' extracurricular activities, the ivy still managed to snag the balls.

Even during baseball's great expansion era of the early Sixties, the old parks were still the host to most of the records established in the Senior Circuit. The great Cincinnati Reds' feats belong to Crosley Field, Pirate records were made and broken in Forbes, and most blue-blooded Dodger fans still believe their team's greatest traditions belonged with Ebbets Field until time and performance made the Los Angeles Dodgers a force to be reckoned with in Chavez Ravine.

No one except the mosquitoes seemed to miss Houston's old Colts Field. Feeling nostalgic about that place was like feeling nostalgic about the bubonic plague. Day or night games there were always a hazardous affair.

A summer afternoon at Colts Field meant being bleached by an unmerciful sun. At night, herds of giant, prehistoric mosquitoes converged on the park for feeding time. The climate vacillated between the daytime Sahara in the nighttime Everglades.

Baseball is a game that is necessarily laden with statistics. It is the fundamental device that gauges performance and establishes records. They categorize and rank performances in a hierarchy, and is the common language that transcends baseball from the time of Miller Huggins to Dwight Gooden.

When I retired in 1982, after 20 seasons, there were several umpiring records I toted off the field with my back that last game. But umpires *work* games, they do not *play* them and consequently, their retinue of individual records is limited. Usually their records are inexorably tied-in with players' performances. An umpire can boast he called balls and strikes during a perfect game or that he had field duty when Joe Palooka broke the record for the most home runs hit in a single game. But these are instances when umpires are present at the creation of a player's new record. Rarely are umpires' records apart from players' records.

An ump can lay claim to the fact that he officiated the longest game in baseball history, but any man on either team can claim to have played in the longest game in baseball history.

There are a couple of records I've accumulated as an umpire that are totally apart from the performance of any player or team. To the best of my knowledge, I am the only major league umpire to have ever vomited on home plate in the glorious history of baseball. This is no small honor considering that besides being the judges and arbitrators on the field, umpires are also the janitors, custodians, and general stewards of home plate aesthetics. When the baseball Hall of Fame decides to build that long-awaited ward called the Hall of Dubious Honors, I know this incident will someday be enshrined in Cooperstown forever.

I had the home plate assignment for a Dodgers-Milwaukee Braves game at Chavez Ravine in 1964. On the flight from Chicago, I was hungry and ate a meal that would have killed a brontosaurus. I was sick as soon as I landed in Los Angeles, but come hell or high water, I was determined to be behind the plate in Dodger Stadium with my shin pads, steel-toed shoes and facemask.

I think that in my twenty regular seasons and seventeen games in the majors, I missed only about twenty games. But missing a home plate assignment was not only a letdown to me, but a let down to my crew. It was akin to the captain of the ship leaving all hands plus the women and children on board while he escaped in the first lifeboat.

I contacted Dr. Wood in Los Angeles who managed to tell me something I already knew. I had a genuine case of food poisoning. He advised me not to work the Dodger game and instructed me to rest for the next 24 hours. The doctor was totally unfazed when I told him it was my turn behind the plate. Maybe it was sound medical advice, maybe the doctor was a Dodger fan and didn't want me near Chavez Ravine that night, but I was still determined to be behind the plate at game time.

All of my noble thoughts were much easier said than done. I felt as though the War of the Worlds was being waged between my neck and legs. My eyesight and judgment weren't impaired and other than wishing I could relax in the men's room for a few hours, I thought I was still calling a good game.

The fateful sixth inning proved to be my stomach's undoing. It seemed to happen so quickly. Within seconds I knew what was happening and what was soon going to happen on the Dodger turf. I felt like the loneliest guy in the world. Fans at Chavez Ravine and across the country would see me embarrass myself. There was no time nor any place to hide as I involuntarily bent over home plate and ralphed – over *my* home plate, no less!

Vin Scully announced to the world that it was the first time an umpire vomited on home plate in major league history. Del Crandell of the Braves was at bat, John Roseboro was catching and Johnny Padres was on the mound. None of them could believe their eyes. After the bucket brigade restored home plate to its normal condition, I resumed my position.

Johnny Padres looked me over thoroughly when he stepped into the batters' box in the sixth inning. "I wasn't pitching that bad, was I?" he asked. Del Crandell told me after the game that he thought I must have eaten an entire cornfield before work.

It was bad enough that I vomited in front of everyone in Dodger Stadium and television land, but when Leo Durocher knew, I was in for a rocky future. Leo had the memory of a bull elephant and was not above firing any unpleasant information he could muster right into an umpire's face.

On my next trip to Dodger Stadium, Leo happen to be coaching third base. In the 10th inning, he began to chant some ugly cognates from the coaching box about a called strike on Ron Fairly. I knew all too well that there was only one way to handle Durocher when he was in a cranky mood. I looked him squarely in the eyes and yelled, "Aaaaaaah, shut up!"

Leo replied to my thoughtful suggestion with a litany of dangling similes. When I heard enough, I threw him out of the game. But Leo was never able to quietly retire to the showers. The image of me vomiting on home plate came to his bald mind. He ran to home plate where I was positioned holding his throat and choking desperately. "Why don't you go drink some more green Irish beer," he screamed. His pantomime on the field was hilarious, but I certainly didn't appreciate his comment. It was already months after St. Patrick's Day!

Because of my inglorious moment behind the plate that night in Dodger Stadium, Leo permanently dubbed me "The Puker." Unfortunately, it was the only nickname in my life that ever stuck.

In 1975, I umpired two games in two separate cities in one day. This task would have been impossible before baseball teams and umpires shuffled from city to city by air. Statisticians have no interest or no established category for this hybrid feat, but amongst umpires it is something of a benchmark.

I had just finished working a day game in Candlestick Park when the National League offices contacted me to work a game that night at Dodgers Stadium. Ed Sudol was a member of the umpiring crew in Los Angeles and had just received word that afternoon that his father died in New Jersey. The National League mullahs wanted to know if I could leave San Francisco right away on a flight to Los Angeles, five hundred miles away. "What the hell," I told them, "I'll just chalk this up as part of the craziness of the trade."

I arrived at Dodgers Stadium and joined Ed's crew for a game between the Dodgers and Cubs. Because I was either the odd man in or the odd man out of this umpiring crew, I was kindly given rocking chair duty on the third base line. The game turned out to be a classic pitchers' duel. Both Sandy Koufax for the Dodgers and Bob Henley of the Cubs were masterful. Their pitches were working magically on the mound as batters on both teams were routinely swinging in the breeze. Fate had directed me to a very special game that night. It turned out to be one of the three perfect games in National League history.

Glenn Beckert of the Cubs had a shot that I called foul on the third base line. It barely twisted foul by two inches and kept Chicago off the bases. Henley pitched a marvelous one-hitter but Koufax was barely, barely, one hit better.

Politicians are more generous about naming new rules after their sponsors than just about any other profession I can imagine. Most people may not know anything about the Taft-Hartley Act, but they know at least that a Mr. Taft and a Mr. Hartley were in some way, behind it. The new Graham-Rudman-Hollings bill that requires a balanced federal budget by 1990 is another classic example. No one knows how the nation's coffers will be balanced, but at least we know who sponsored the legislation.

Official baseball is not as lavish in bestowing umpires' names to new rules added to the book. New rules will always be instituted in baseball simply because of the nature of the sport. Unpredictable events occur during the course of a season that are not accounted for by any official rule. There are 88 keys on a piano, but the number of variations in song are as numerous as the stars. The official rules handily account for the probable instances, and it even gives an umpire an extension to his own common sense in making an unusual call, but men will be boys and events will occur on the field that will befuddle the most arduous Rule Book scholar.

I watched with a foot-long face as Jimmy Piersall ran around the bases backwards. The Rule Book indicates that a player cannot run the bases in reverse order to reach home plate, but there is no rule about a nut who travels the base paths with a southern exposure. The only rule I had at my disposal with Piersall was to fine him for making a travesty of the sport. I didn't think it was a travesty – but I did think it was damn funny. I didn't fine Jimmy for his unusual victory lap.

Every veteran umpire has made calls on the field without any pertinent rule. Even after the decision has been recorded by journalists and accepted by baseball's mullahs, rarely, if ever, does an umpire get the new rule named after him. This was always a let down to the umpiring profession because instead of taking five minutes to explain a new rule call to a manager, you could save time and money by just invoking the Pryor Rule, or the Donatelli Rule or the Secory Rule to that particular instance.

During one game I umpired in 1968 at Candlestick Park between the Giants and the Braves, an interesting scenario took place that later did change the rulebook. Atlanta's Norm Larker was on third base when Ty Cline came up to bat. The Braves tried a suicide squeeze play to bring Larker home. Cline bunted a pitch that nearly became an infield fly. Ed Bailey of the Giants chased the hit and positioned himself right in the middle of the base path to home to field the ball.

Norm Larker arrived at a great idea on his winged way to home plate. Bailey looked pleasantly positioned under the ball to make a convenient catch and after that probably had pressing thoughts to throw to the plate. Larker decided to liquidate the possibility of either play. Without stepping outside the base path, he bowled Bailey over before he could catch the ball. This looked like a maneuver that should only be performed by stuntmen or roller derby people.

I called Cline out because of Larker's interference with Bailey. It was a very catchable catch and I thought Larker should have attempted to move around him on his way towards the plate. Top of that, I called Norm Larker out because, in all likelihood, Bailey's catch and an easy flip to third base would have caught Larker scurrying back to the bag. Besides, Bailey was lucky he was knocked off his rocker and not deposited clear into next week.

The Atlanta bench had absolutely no sense of humor about my call. My decision was the talk of the announcers' booths and the nation's sportswriters that night and for the next few. Enough discussion seemed to have been generated in professional baseball circles that the leagues' autocrats decided to investigate the matter of making a definitive rule for such situations. Shortly afterwards, a new rule was added to baseball's legislation. A player could not physically prevent a man from making a catch in his direct line of run on the base path. The rules of the road belonged to the defensive player in this instance.

A dugout is the privileged domain of the team's players. It is their encampment beside the field and it is guarded with the same fervor as a zealot's territorial instincts for the sanctum sanctorum. As a cardinal rule (or even a blue jay or oriole one for that matter), the dugout is partial only to the particular players and personnel it is designated to host. Even umpires are calibans if they abuse the sanctity of this special estate. The sudden appearance of an opposing player in its confines is nearly tantamount to a declaration of war.

No other professional sport quarters their players in any kind of structure that even remotely resembles a dugout. Only in baseball are participants shielded from the stands and elements by these unusual warrens representing shoeboxes carved into the architecture of the stadium complex.

An opposing fielder frequently finds a dugout to be a no man's land full of traps and snares like gloves, masks, and shin pads strewn about its entrance. Fortunately, it's usually only catchers and first and third baseman who ever find themselves in the precarious position of entering the mouth of the enemy's cave to catch wayward foul balls.

For nearly all of baseball's history, an opposing fielder entered a dugout at his own risk to life and limb. Not only did he have to delicately prance between the sundry items of equipment, jeers from bench jockeys, but he ran the hazard of being robbed of a particularly catchable catch.

During one interesting game in 1964 between the Phillies and the Mets, I made a controversy call that helped inaugurate a new dugout rule. The mores of dugout antics were permanently changed thereafter.

Jerry Grote was catching for the Mets when a high popup foul arched toward the Phillies' dugout. He was planted on the first step and in perfect form for the ball to drop directly in his glove. Just before the foul reached his mitt, however, Philadelphia manager Gene Mauch leaned forward towards Grote and knocked his glove arm down. Jerry stood in the Philly dugout looking like the jilted groom at a wedding.

I called a "catch" because Grote would have made the grab without Mauch's assistance. He had reached the foul in sufficient time to have handily made a routine catch. Had all conditions of the hit been duplicated and the Mets' dugout juxtaposed with that of the Phillies, I'm sure Grote would have made his snag. Mauch and the rest of the Phillies, the announcers, and the press were flabbergasted with my call. Curt Gowdy called the field ruling a mistake.

I mulled over my decision for the rest of the game. After weighing both sides, there seemed to be more reasons in support of my call than against it. The ability of an opposing player or manager to disrupt the fielding of dugout balls seemed arcane. Baseball laws have been made to deal with fans interrupting a defensive player from properly executing a play. Why shouldn't a defensive player be protected in the enemy dugout? It seemed a miracle that more accidents didn't occur during dugout catches. Dugout players could scream and crowd him out of his concentration. Worse than that, he could be physically robbed of a catch during a crucial game that might determine a pennant race or World Series.

My decision created such a brouhaha amongst the high mugwamps of baseball that a new rule was finally created. Any defense man attempting to field a ball in or immediately before the dugout must be provided with sufficient room to adequately play the ball. I'm convinced it's a good role for baseball despite whatever Curt Gowdy happens to think about the sad loss of rock 'em, sock 'em and baseball!

Most four-man umpiring crews have a member who is the extra inning jinx. Those crews without one usually acquire a jinx when a substitute umpire from another crew happens to join them for a brief interlude. Nobody knows what strange alchemy the jinx unwittingly bestows, nor can anyone be sure exactly when the Muse of Extra Innings taps him on his shoulder with her wand to make a "normal" nine inning game become a "long day's journey into night."

Until the National League decided to mix and match personnel instead of maintaining the old system of membership, it was easy to determine the jinx on the field. Most of the time, it was the newest addition to the crew. The more superstitious umpires did not attribute extra inning ordeals to the conduct and circumstances of the game. The crew's jinx was mystically responsible for prolonging the game. No one could adequately explain the reason why someone was a jinx, it was more a sixth sense the umpire had that determined the culprit. Usually the jinx himself was totally unaware of his strange powers until he was informed about it by other members of the crew.

He was just the jinx and nobody could explain it. The poor guy may have had third base duty for a game and not made a call at the bag or over the foul line, but the game had been dragged into extra innings because he was on the field. It was just that simple.

Extra inning free-for-alls are customarily anathema to umpires. It's not so much the fact that the crew has to work any longer on the field, but airline reservations to the next city and equipment pick-ups have to be altered. On a number of occasions, my crews were so delayed because of extra-inning games that the only way we could make game time in the next city on the following day was to book passage on a magic carpet.

My first major league plate assignment was a sixteen inning extravaganza between the Pirates and Phillies Connie Mack Stadium. This was not a good omen for the veteran umpires of the crew I just joined. Frank Secory, Augie Donatelli, and Tony Venson somehow felt I was so happy to be in the majors that I magically prolonged the game. They wondered if this was going to be the kind of luck I was bringing to the crew.

Wes Covington of the Phillies finally entered the batters' box in the 16th inning and hit Johnny Buzhard. Two games jammed into one was beginning to be a bit much for my first game in the majors. Luckily for the crew and my green, rookie neck, Covington hit the ball and the Phillies finally prevailed.

"Kid, you did a good job," Augie Donatelli told me in the umpires' locker room after the game. "But you didn't have to keep us out there after nine innings. And you sure as hell didn't have to keep us out there for sixteen innings!"

Somehow I drew home plate duty for my second game in the majors. Fortunately, it was a "normal" nine inning game and I thank my lucky stars for that. I really didn't want to be the crew's extra-inning magus.

I played that season's remaining seventeen games with my crew and tried to discourage players from getting any bright ideas for putting games beyond God's allotted nine innings. During the off-season, I paid particular attention to any omens like strange laughter in the dark or things that went bump in the night. I joined Augie, Frank Secory, and Tony Venson again in 1962 for the opening game of spring training's Grapefruit League in Florida. Just when the crew was beginning to forget about my credentials as the extra-inning jinx – it happened again. A twelve inning spring training ordeal between the Pirates and the Phillies confirmed any of my crew members' lingering doubts. I was the jinx of the four umps on the field. The other crew members just looked at me after the game and shook their heads in disgust.

But if I was truly an extra-inning provocateur, I at least wanted some long records to share with my fairy godmother. I retired from professional baseball as one of four umpires to have officiated the longest game in big league history. For seven hours and 43 minutes, Ed Sudol, Bill Jackowski, Chris Pelakoudas and I were camped at Shea Stadium for a marathon duel between the Mets and the Giants. It proved a great conversational piece for banquet speeches. When little leaguers looked up to me and asked, "What did you do in the majors for 20 years?" I could always tell them about the thrill and excitement of umpiring the longest game.

It was the second game of a doubleheader started at 4 PM at Shea. By the time we reached the dressing rooms, our plane had departed hours earlier. We were scheduled to be in Chicago the next day to work a game at Wrigley Field. The crew didn't have accommodations for the night and most of the hotels outside of the wino havens were booked solid because of the World's Fair.

Jackie Gleason was at Shea Stadium for the game and dropped by the umpires' locker room to meet us. He overheard the problem of our housing dilemma and offered us a night's lodging in his suite at the Park Sheridan in Manhattan. We didn't want to disappoint him. How many times has he had the opportunity to share his abode with four major league umpires? We took him up on his offer and spent the night in Jackie's luxurious suite. The next day we were on a 9 o'clock flight for O'Hare managed to be at Wrigley Field dressed for game time.

Ed Sudol had worked a seventeen inning marathon on the Thursday preceding our record breaker. In just those two games he worked about forty innings of baseball. The crew received a nice letter from National League president Warren Giles thanking us for not walking off the field in the long Mets-Giants game. He sent a check to help us celebrate this extraordinary gain. All four of us went out on the town – all because Ed Sudol decided to keep us on the field for so long.

Exactly whoever or whatever hovered above the field certainly took a disliking to me. I was getting known around both leagues for my extra-inning shenanigans. On each occasion I was behind the plate for the 1967, 1973, and 1980 World Series, I somehow managed to have the longest game of each Series. My evil genie must have been testing me during the 1967 Cards-Red Sox Series when I called balls and strikes in size 9 ½ shoes.

My Mets-Giants long-game credentials were sadly destroyed in 1985 when a new time record was established for a game. It broke my heart to see my claim to fame blemished by a new record. I had to even revamp my after-dinner speeches. Evidently, the Force that was once within me had departed for greater ballparks and I felt like a lesser umpire because of it.

By the time the official 1961 season ended, I had umpired only about seventeen major league games. This was hardly enough experience to even talk shop with the men who had just completed a full rookie year. With only one season of triple-A ball behind me, I was definitely a greenhorn in the majors. In order to gain more experience, Warren Giles asked me to work in the Puerto Rican leagues during the winter of 1961. The following winter the league sent me down again to the Caribbean for another dose of Amigo baseball. Because I was a major leaguer, albeit one still very wet behind the ears, I was made an umpire-in-chief of the leagues for the 1962 winter. I was going to run a crew of six Puerto Ricans and three American umpires that season.

The idea of working and living on the island seemed great. I was going to avoid the North American winter and umpire in sun kissed, Caribbean ballparks. Coconut palms were supposed to tilt gently beyond the outfield fences in the balmy trade winds breezes. I had heard vicious stories about the Latin American leagues, but I attributed them to products of the rumor mill.

Other umpires and players who had spent a season in the Latin leagues told me outrageous stories of the militia in combat gear entering ballparks to quell a potential revolution. Outfield walls crashed down as angry mobs ransacked the field. Umpires barricaded themselves in their locker room while they waited for the siege to be lifted by the militia. I still chalked-up their stories as exaggerations. How could baseball get more out of hand that beer night in a minor league park? How could the Puerto Rican fans possibly compare to the Philly Fanatics or the Bleacher Bums on a good day at Wrigley Field?

It took only a couple of games to realize that all the horror tales were true. Saying that the Puerto Rican fans were more temperamental than their American counterparts is like saying that the Huns were slightly more excitable than Quakers. I used to think it was a tough night back home when beer and Coney Island T-bones rained on the field. That was child's play in Puerto Rico. Hard objects were thrown at umpires, designed to either shatter on impact or shatter them. It was horrifying to understand what the fans wanted to do to the umpires following a call they disagreed with. This was like officiating in the reactivated Devil's Island. Baseball was never meant to be played like this!

The league was comprised of six teams. The smaller cities of Ponce, Arecibo, Mayaguez, and Caracas each had a team, while bustling San Juan was the home of two clubs. Theoretically, moving between the cities during the course of the winter season should not have been difficult. Puerto Rico is only 131 miles long by 44 miles wide. You can't move around that much without having your hat float. Depending upon where we just finished one game and what city was next on our itinerary, the crew frequently took a taxi.

Winter is not the only time for baseball in Puerto Rico, but it is also the tourist season. What better time is there for the taxi drivers to go out on strike? Instead of hopping a cab to the next city in 1962, we were forced to ride the infamous "publicos." These are the open cars that look like San Franciscan trolleys without the rails. The drivers had great senses of humor. They thought it was funny to speed around the island like Richard Petty while everyone held on for dear life. There was no designated capacity and the publicos picked-up everybody. I mean *everybody*. This made for particularly the interesting traveling companions.

The publico would stop at designated places to pick-up and discharge passengers. If people were jammed inside the publico and others hung on the outside railing and climbed to the top of the cab – that was no problem. More people would just climb aboard at the stop and the driver would attempt to move from 0 to 60 mph in five seconds.

I picked up one publico in San Juan to umpire the next game in Ponce. I rode the entire distance next to a thoughtful woman who decided to bring her two chickens along for the ride. I couldn't eat a drumstick or think about Frank Perdue for a long while after that episode.

There are basically two types of baseball fans in Puerto Rico. There are the rabid fans and then there are the "fanaticos." Both flavors are slightly more temperamental than their counterparts in the States. During their unusual fits of good behavior, the rabid fans are still several decibels above Chicago's Bleacher Bombs on a crazy day. They shout, scream, throw things and each other onto the playing field. Basically, they're great baseball fans with a rowdy factor squared. The fanaticos are just dangerous. They charge up to the playing field en masse and really want to tear the umpires apart. Fanaticos do not bathe officials with beer or pelt them with the blunt ends of hot dogs. Many of these hombres carry guns and knives. They make Philly Fanatics and Bleacher Bums look like Casper Milquetoasts.

Sometimes the only effective deterrent to a fanatico rampage is the presence of the army. While the National Guard in the US is kept busy with natural disasters like hurricanes and floods, the Guard in Puerto Rico is activated for baseball games. The sight of soldiers in olive drabs with combat boots, helmets and big guns inside a baseball stadium is an unusual sight. During my season as umpire-in-chief, I frequently looked at the stands from my position on the field toward a long line of soldiers with automatic rifles – and was damned grateful they were there!

Once in Arecibo, and the frenzied mob of fanaticos outside the stadium decided to vent their frustration inside the park. The outfield wall came crashing down as packs of fanaticos charged onto the field. Even the hometown players weren't safe. No prisoners would be taken among the ranks of umpires. It was every umpire for himself – kill or be killed. Doug Harvey and I were running a brisk Mach 8 and edging toward the speed of light in our dash to the locker rooms. Frank Howard happened to be a Winter Leaguer that year. When the fanaticos stormed onto the field, Frank took pity on a Puerto Rican umpire. He ran up to the terrified official, picked them up as if he was a small department store mannequin and carried him back to the safety of the locker room. It took about an hour before the fanaticos outside our barricaded door finally dispersed.

The island experience taught me a little lesson in baseball and history. If the Romans only had fans like the fanaticos for their Coliseum games, the Vandals would never have stood a barbarian's chance.

Unlike the Puerto Rican leagues, security at major league stadiums is customarily excellent. The fool or fanatic that prances on the field is usually apprehended quickly and escorted either outside the portals or to the crossbar hotel without untimely delays in the game. But it's always interesting to speculate on the motives of the men and women who dash clothed or unclothed onto the playing field. Some people, no doubt, consider a nationally televised game as a perfect medium for an agentless audition for the $1.98 Beauty Contest or an evening with David on the David Letterman show. Other cheap thrill seekers may flaunt their wares on a dare from friends, the result of too many trips to the beer stands, or just because they are bona fide nuts.

I umpired a game in Philadelphia when a political rally was staged on the field. Cookie Rojas came to bat for the Phillies when a group of Cuban-Americans jumped the rail and ran out on the diamond to protest the Castro regime.

During and Atlanta Braves' game, Clete Boyer encountered Morgana, the buxom, kissing bandit in the batter's box. She ran onto the field and planted a few passionate kisses on Clete when he was just getting ready to bat. Boyer managed to hit a double that the fans attributed to Morgana's caresses. They demanded that this gangster of love be allowed to return to the field to kiss the next Brave hitter for good measure. Lusty Calls for Morgana filled Fulton County Stadium while the attendants continued to escort her out of the complex.

While my formal umpire's judgment may frown on streakers and their naked antics on the field, there's a part of me that found streaking entertaining – that is, if it was a woman on the field. Fortunately, as an umpire, I've never had to chase a naked person around the park. Perhaps his duty was assigned to the stadium attendants because official baseball felt umpires wouldn't know what to do with a naked, fleet-of-foot philly when she was captured on the field.

I had second base duty at Dodger Stadium in 1982 when I caught the image of a fan on the field out of the corner of my eye. Whoever had just entered the field was making a beeline for my area of the diamond. Whether it was Mr. T or Pollyanna, I couldn't tell, but I hustled out of the way of what seemed to be a collision course between me and the unidentified flying person.

I managed to get closer to second base before I turned around. An attractive, fully-clothed young woman was standing very close to Fernando Valenzuela on the mound. She looked as if she was kissing Fernando, so I immediately moved in the direction of the pitcher's mound for a closer look. My first thought after I reach the periphery of the mound was "Gee, the gal must really like Fernando!" She reached the maximum limits of what someone could amorously do in a ballpark without disrobing. She nibbled on his lips, flicked her tongue in and out of his ear, kissed him on the mouth and had a case of that foreign love ailment known as Russian Hands and Roman Fingers.

If Fernando liked this special treatment, he contained his emotions. But he certainly didn't raise a hand to brush her off. I think the rookies in the dugout must have blushed. Amorous displays like this don't occur too often in the bush leagues.

The next day, the sports section of the Los Angeles times ran a photo of Fernando, the sexcited young woman, and me, staring dumbfounded on the mound. The caption poignantly captured the essence of the moment: "Umpire Paul Pryor never misses a play." They're damned right.

Irate players and managers usually charge out of dugouts under the influence of what I call "instant" anger." This is the involuntary variety of being p.o.'ed. The mind's eye takes in an outrageous event and tells the player's legs to propel him in front of the umpire's face. Mean syllables are unabashedly created by the brain and immediately disposed of by the mouth. This is an instinctive, spontaneous human reaction.

In most cases, instant anger is the predecessor to creative – when a player or manager actively plans a malicious act against an umpire. For example, Leo Durocher can watch a call from the dugout that he disagrees with. As soon as his bald head registers disagreement, he is on his feet and barking in an umpire's face. Once he detects the fact that his argument has absolutely no effect on the ump and may even get him thrown out of the game, Leo's mind shifts gears to creative anger (tantamount in most cases to tantrums). It is at this point that furtive little plans for retaliation are being hatched beneath his chrome dome. He may kick there, throw his hat in the air, pick-up a base and walk away with it, or do just about anything to boil an umpire's blood.

Players are frequently as unpredictable as their pitches and hits. An umpire can rely on the rulebook as well as his own judgment and common sense as a guide to make calls on the field, but dealing with a player in the throes of creative anger can be another matter altogether. There is a certain glint that suddenly flashes in his eyes to register both anger and mischevy. It is the sort of look that unmistakably communicates reprisal. Without words, it is his way of saying, "Okay, ump, you just called me out, but I've got a couple of tricks up my sleeve and let's see how you like it!"

Once at Three Rivers Stadium, I called Richie Hebner out on strikes when he was playing for the Pittsburgh Pirates. Richie glared at me in anger and began the motion of throwing his bat in the air. I anticipated his move and cautioned him, "If you throw that bat and it just happens to land on the ground, I'm finding you $100."

Hebner not only flipped his bat in the air, but it came down. He was so disgusted with my call that he marched to the dugout and proceeded to throw all the Pirates' bats and equipment onto the field. I began counting the items fired out of the dugout and registered them in the hundreds of dollars. But instead of taking a strict accounting of all of bats, face masks, shin pads, and batting helmets cascading out of the dugout, I lost count after four items and $400 and continued to watch the dugout as it was depleted of equipment. I decided to find Hebner $100 and throw him out of the park. Immediately after the game I intended to write a report to National League President Chubb Feeney explaining Hebner's actions as well as my recommended fine.

Pirates Manager Danny Murtaugh approached me and demanded to know why Hebner was ejected from the game. Through a spray of amber tobacco juice, he claimed that the fine for throwing any item on the field was $100, not ejected from the game.

I looked at the bric-a-brac strewn in front of the Pirates' dugout and then slowly turned back to Murtaugh. "I'm throwing him out because if I counted all the stuff on the field and find him, I'd send him home broke."

People who charge out of dugouts usually are the bearers of bad tidings. Managers ready to blow their head gaskets and distraught players are difficult enough for the umpire to deal with, but by far the worst thing exiting the dugout at high speed is a team stampeding into a fight.

I've been involved in eight or nine bench-clearing brawls during my 20 years in the National League. This averages out to one healthy donnybrook every other season or so. Although this can still be exasperating for an umpire, at least in American and Canadian baseball a full-pledged brouhaha involves players battling other players. An umpire should try to break-up a fight, but when both teams clear the dugouts and clean each other's clocks on the field, the best course of action is sometimes to stay out of it.

Brawls in Latin American baseball are downright unhealthy for umpires. There, an umpire does not so much fear a bench-clearing brawl, than a stadium-clearing fight where more than frequently the umpires are the source of fan frustration. When the spectators evacuate stands faster than during a fire drill and reach the playing field – that is the umpires' subtle cue to move from 0 to 60 mph and head for their locker room before bath time.

Most brawls in the majors are the result of a bean ball pitch, a hard slide into a base in the ensuing dispute or just bench jockeying from the opposing team. The whole world can watch a close or disputed play on the bases, but fans are seldom privy to bench jockeying from the dugouts. Unless fans are seated beside the dugout, they rarely hear the choice expletive deletives and comments tossed at opposing pitchers and batters. Everything from their funny looks to the size of their wives' derrières is criticized from the dugout. But a brawl caused by bench carolers often appears to be a case of spontaneous combustion for most fans in the stands and in television land. Both dugouts magically clear in seconds for a melee caused by something only players and team personnel seem to understand.

I was on umpiring a game at Shea Stadium in 1968 between the Giants and Mets when a real hay burner erupted in the field. Tito Fuentes of the Giants slid into second and was tagged by Felix Milan. I called Fuentes out and as I began to walk away, I noticed that both players were kidding each other about the play. Milan and Fuentes had smiles on their faces and seems to be engaged in a case of gentle ribbing. I took a few more steps and turned around to position myself for the next play when I saw Fuentes and Milan beating each other up over second base. I ran over to both players and told them to knock off the gladiator show. There was a ten second cease and desist before both guys again started to reconstruct each other's faces. This second bout became the curtain call for both benches to evacuate their dugouts and wage war on the diamond.

Once the flood gates are open and both teams begin their donnybrook, the best thing an umpire can do is stand sway until the dust has settled before ejecting the instigators. It is better to be a peacemaker than a brawler, but better to retain thine natural good looks and return to the umpires' locker room with a face resembling a meat pie in search of a crust. To thine own God-given face be true becomes the axiom of the moment. Sometimes a conscious effort to avoid the flying knuckles and knees works to no avail. I left the Fuentes-Milan fight and returned to the officials' corner with a ripped shirt and scratches on my face.

Another memorable and painful dugout clearer involved the Dodgers and Giants. San Francisco's Jack Sanford through a pitch that seemed to be designed to remove the five o'clock shadow from Willie Crawford's face. He began to charge the mound with his bat in hand when he was tackled by catcher Jack Hyatt from behind. Crawford still had his bat in hand when Hyatt did his impressive imitation of a middle linebacker. No sooner did Crawford and Hyatt hit the infield turf when both benches unloaded and beat each other up for a few minutes.

There are a number of interesting people and objects that fall out of the stands onto the playing field. Some things like chicken bones, beer, beer cups, half-eaten hotdogs, toilet paper, ball bearing, and size D batteries are mischievously thrown at players and umpires by fans who are either perturbed about a play or are taking some joyful target practice.

Bob Uecker and I remember one incident at Veterans Stadium that should somehow be commemorated in the Hall of Fame. I had home plate duty for a Phillies' game when a fan fell from the upper deck and live to tell about it!

At the time, I only noticed a ruckus in the lower deck and assumed it was one of the usual local fights amongst Philly fans and friends. Shortly afterward, I was informed that a guy had tumbled out of the upper deck without suffering any real injuries. Suddenly the episode became comical.

Evidently, the guy had performed the dual feat of falling from the upper deck without killing himself and landing without forcibly shortening any of the unsuspecting fans below. This is a one-in-a-billion accomplishment. But on top of all that, Bob Uecker noticed the fans' reaction to this guy who was suddenly catapulted in their midst. Instead of having sympathy and concern for the fallen fan, his obtrusive and uninvited presence disturbed their viewing of the game. The fans around called him a bum and started to pelt them with popcorn and stadium trash for falling from the sky without a proper calling card! Better here than in Philadelphia.

No player likes to be called out. It's a part of the human condition that will never change. Some players respect and umpire's call matter how they may disagree with it and returned to the dugout to think about their next time at bat or their next catch in the field. Others reject the call and insist on putting the monkey on the umpire's back. In my time, I've carried many of the animal kingdom's great apes piggyback.

There is a lot of pressure on professional ballplayers to deliver, particularly in situations with men on base in scoring position. Sometimes when I've called players out on strikes in the late innings with men on the base paths and the team down a run or two, I've had to listen to comments like, "You're taking the bat out of my hands!" "You're taking away my bread and butter," was another popular retort. This is always a hard one for me to be sympathetic about because their salaries look like long distance phone numbers.

While Bob Uecker claims that the "fans never forget you" – there is an entirely different case for umpires. Old umps may fade in the memories of fans, but the ballplayers never forget them. Some players will hold grudges that carry over from season to season, year after year.

I called Felix Mantilla out on strikes on one occasion in 1963 and when I happened to meet him off the field in 1967, he recited that earlier event verse, line, and syllable. He told me he was up in the third inning of the game and the third called strike was a foot outside of the strike zone. They never forget when they're supposed to deliver with men on the bases.

When I was umpire-in-chief of the Puerto Rican League in 1962, I officiated one memorable game with Bob Gibson on the mound. The Ron Rico Rum Company offered a standing challenge throughout the winter of a $1000 cash prize to anyone who pitched a no-hitter. During most of the game, it appeared as though Gibson was on his way to a cool Caribbean grand. Batters were routinely swinging and missing. The defense was successful in catching everything that was hit. Just when it appeared that Gibson may have had a game clenched, Marv Breeding, the Baltimore Orioles second baseman managed to get an infield hit and then barely beat the throw to first. Gibson was infuriated with my call and thought Breeding was out by at least a mile or two. Bob was out a fast thousand he thought he deserved from Ron Rico, Breeding wasn't out on first, and I became a Gibson outcast for the next year or so.

Many devoted baseball buffs seem to take almost a proprietary interest in how their favorite team's fans are perceived by umpires and other players. Life in the other stadiums is still very much a mystery to most baseballphiles. I'm frequently asked questions like, "Who are the rowdiest fans in the National

League?" "Who are the most knowledgeable fans in the Senior Circuit?" "In terms of fans, when parks are the hardest and easiest to umpire?" Often the seemingly naïve questions are asked by people who are walking baseball compendiums. But unless they've spent time in other major league parks, they are not particularly aware of how fans in other stadiums conduct themselves.

New York fans are very knowledgeable about baseball and especially their Mets, but there is an unpredictable element about them. They can be mysteriously understanding about a call on the field one moment and then invite you to a necktie party the next.

Usually when I umpired a game in New York, I would take the subway to Flushing Meadows for the game. If it was a day game on a weekend, the entire families would ride the train together to Shea Stadium. Fathers, mothers, sons, and daughters talked baseball throughout the subway ride. They knew all about Ed Kranepool, Choo-Choo Coleman, Tom Seaver, and the other Amazing Mets. They could recite batting averages, slugging percentages, and the ERAs of their Mets. Fathers would quiz sons about the statistics and sons would test their fathers about the career records of their favorite players. But make a call the Met fans didn't like and they're prepared to draw and quarter an umpire in Times Square at high noon.

I remember in 1968 I worked the third base line in the game between the Mets and St. Louis Cardinals at Shea Stadium. I called out New York's Wayne Garrett in a close play at the bag. Whatever amiability I noticed on the subway ride that day to the stadium was instantly lost. The entire ballpark became rabid. A few moments after I called Garrett out and the game resumed, I noticed piles of chicken bones around third base. I bent down and started to pick-up the remnants of a chicken feast and became infuriated. I wasn't particularly mad because the fans were upset over my call at third and started throwing things at me, that's part of the hazards of the profession. What incensed me was that the fans had the audacity to throw chicken on the field without leaving even a measly scrap of meat on any of the bare bones. Now that's a real insult!

Met fans are candidates for the Nobel Peace Prize compared to Philly roosters. Many of the Veterans Stadium devotees believe that the only kind of good umpire is a dead one. They hate everything about umpires – they hate the reasons why we even exist – they hate our looks, they hate where we're from, they hate our families, and they especially hate a call against their team.

But while Philly fans are the rowdiest in the National League, they are perhaps the most knowledgeable baseball fans. That's both good and bad. It's nice to know that so many of the people that file into Veterans Stadium are such baseball enthusiasts, but it has a tendency to make them browbeat their own players almost as much as they harass umpires. They know statistical histories of the Phillies and sometimes ride a player if he is not playing up to his past records and their expectations. I've been in veterans Stadium when Philadelphia greats like Mike Schmidt and Del Ennis struck out and the fans have screamed for them to be hung from Independence Hall by their thumbs. Native Philadelphians have told me that Philly fans can become so irate with their team that they travel to International Airport when they are on the road just to boo the party planes.

Umpires also have to watch their P's and Q's at Wrigley Field. The "Bleacher Bums" are die-hard Cubby fans and they know their baseball inside and out. But after a number of beer runs to the concession stands and basking in the hot prairie son, any kind of mischief is possible from the guys in the cheap seats.

I umpired a game between Los Angeles and Chicago at Wrigley Field one afternoon when Frank Howard was playing in the outfield for the Dodgers. Billy Williams had a fly near the ivy wall in front of the Bums. Frank was positioned under the ball and poised for the catch and some of the Bums decided to baptize him in a cold beer bath. Howard missed the catch and Billy Williams began running the bases while several of the Bums took great pride in their offense of assistance to the Cubbies. I saw what happened in the outfield to Frank Howard's "catchable catch" and called the runner out. Wrigley Field broke into an uproar over my call. The Bleacher Bums were ready to jump the wall and extract a few pounds of my flesh in retribution.

Team mascots can be a horrendous nuisance to umpires. These are the characters who wear the colorful Disney-style outfits and parade up and down the roof of their team's dugout leading the cheers. The problem is that too often they encourage fans in their jeers. As master cheerleaders they are also the ringmasters of a potential lynching party.

During a game in San Diego, I became so mad at "The Chicken" that I nearly plucked his feathers and kicked his tail up and down the field. A Padre was up at bat and hit the ball to an infielder. The throw and the tag to first were close, but I called the runner out. The San Diego fans disagreed with my call and wanted to tar and feather me on the spot. Meanwhile, The Chicken started to perform some strange poultry mating dance around me. When he finished this ritual, to the delight of the fans at Jack Murphy Stadium, he squatted down and laid a balloon egg right in front of me. It had been a rough day and this was just a little too much. I wanted to personally escort him to a butcher's shop.

"Why you (dangling participle, mixed, mean metaphors)! I'll give you a kick that'll send you ten feet in the air!" I told him.

It was bad enough that the fans were raising hell in the stands, but The Chicken's encouragement raised the jeers a few more decibels. He finally realized just how mad I was at his shenanigans and apologized after the game.

Fans blame umpires for all sorts of problems. A pitcher may have a bad day largely because of umpires. Batters fall into slumps and runners trip between bases mostly because of umpires. Their physical presence in the stadium alone is responsible for fielders committing errors. Batters are always out because of umpires.

Sometimes fans read strange motives into an umpire's call. It's not just that an ump can be half-blind and all-stupid, as the general consensus seems to maintain, but occasionally a call is attributed to a strange, ulterior motive.

Once in San Francisco, I called Willie Mays out on strikes. A day or two later, I received a call from the Bay Area chapter of the NAACP. Apparently, they had done some research into my career and discovered I taught school in North Carolina. Somehow the connection was made that I called Willie Mays out on strikes because I was a white, Southern umpire. My life in the South was like being the Rhode Island Yankee in Andy of

Mayberry's Court. I was from Woonsocket, Rhode Island. I have an accent is thick as Tip O'Neill's. Anyone who approached me on the subject would instantly tell that I was not only a New Englander, but one who is completely colorblind when it came to baseball players. Willie Mays has known me for about 25 years, but no one asked his opinion about my call either.

Teams adopt all sorts of clever devices to give themselves any kind of an advantage. Each field has its own peculiar nuances and the team's management and grounds keeping crew frequently work in tandem to cut or water the grass to help their players. Even the best of fans who never miss a home game are seldom aware of the subtle, little tricks that can assist the team. This is virtually impossible with domed stadiums and most parks with Astroturf, but certain grounds keeping arrangements can be made on the more traditional parks to have mysterious puddles positioned in suspicious places or have the field smartly cut except for a healthy strip of pasture grass on the infield to slow a burning ground ball.

I always thought it was odd that many Dodger-Giants games in Candlestick Park were equipped with a puddle around first base that look like the Mississippi Delta. Maury Wills didn't seem especially fond of trying to steal second in hip boots. Inquiring into the matter with the Candlestick Park authorities was always futile. The drainage system was on the fritz, the weather was bad and they had a lot of rain – excuses were innumerable. The rest of the field could be as dry as the Sahara desert while the first base rested like an island in the Okefenokee Swamp. Ten-foot wide clouds in Northern California do not usually stop in the wind, drop their load on Candlestick Park's first base and then head east to Nevada. Meanwhile, the Dodgers are in town in Maury Wills is having a gangbuster base stealing season.

The landscape architects at Wrigley Field performed some clever tricks with their lawnmowers. When a good hitting team happened to be in Chicago, I noticed that the grass was immaculately cut and the grounds beautifully manicured except for the grass in the infield. I thought this was unusual and it took me a little while before I noticed that hard infield hits had to pass through the tall grass. By the time they reach the Cubs' shortstop or third baseman, they were no longer hard-hit balls. People have said that the grass is always greener over the septic tank, but that's a little ridiculous.

Many fans are under the impression that umpires frequently socialize with players off the field. Nothing is farther from the truth. After a hot day game in Wrigley Field, no one in any umpiring crew decides to have a post-game brew with "Sarge" Matthews or Ryne Sandberg. Umpires may socialize with players during pre-game warm-ups or practice sessions. A lot of players may talk to you on the field during a pitching change or when they first step into the batter's box, but post-game socializing is usually not wise for either party. There is no baseball rule prohibiting fraternization between umpires and players – it's just a sound policy.

Being an umpire not only entails the built-in hazards of the profession like dealing with irate players and managers, getting hit with runaway pitches and fouls, fans who want you committed to a torture rack, but there are also the off-hours, leisure time risks of the trade.

I've developed my own conduct code for umpires in bars. Whenever and umpiring crew shares a few drinks in a hotel bar, the safest policy is not to tell anyone who or what you are. Paul Pryor's Bar Rule #1 –SOBER PEOPLE DISLIKE UMPIRES ALMOST AS MUCH AS DRUNKS. Usually when an umpire or a crew is discovered in a bar, there soon follows a number of standard arguments, no matter whether the bar is in Los Angeles or New York. Some wise guy always has a timely suggestion like, "Hey, why don't you guys go get a real job!" Bettors who have had a couple of drinks are not above publicly recounting their wagering losses. "I lost ten bucks on that game and it's all because of you and that lousy call you made!" The fewer the number of people who know who you are the better! Home

PAUL PRYOR PHOTO GALLERY

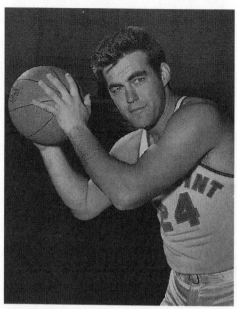

Paul Pryor at High Point College, High Point, N.C.

Semi-pro championship, 1948. Paul Pryor front row, far right

P&Q Shop, Woonsocket, R.I. Coach Roy Sherwood, City League Champions. Paul Pryor front row, second from left

Paul Pryor on right with umpiring crew: Dick Stello, Al Barlick, Ed Vargo,

Frank Walsh, Paul Pryor, Stan Musial, Frank Secory, Ken Burkhart.

Paul Pryor, Dutch Rennert, Bruce Froemming, Harry Wendelstedt, Paul
Runge, Bob Engel

Satch Davidson, Shag Crawford, John Kibler, Paul Pryor

Paul Pryor with wife Carleen at the Stardust in Las Vegas
after the 1962 season

Paul Pryor with Bart Starr on left and son Fred Pryor

Frank Secory, Augie Donatelli, Tony Venson, Paul Pryor

Paul Pryor calls Lou Brock safe in 1967 World Series. Catcher is Boston Red Sox Elson Howard

Paul Pryor watches as Fernando Valenzuela is caressed by the kissing bandit.

Harry Wendelstedt, Ed Sudol, Nick Colosi, Paul Pryor in Philadelphia. His equipment didn't arrive, so Paul Pryor umpired in a make-shift outfit.

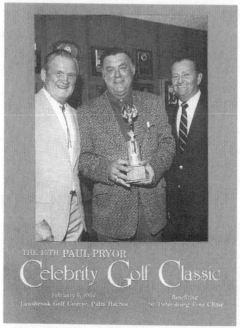

Paul Pryor Celebrity Golf Tournament souvenir program

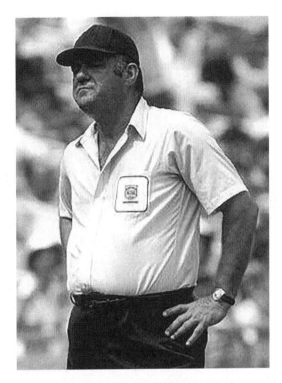

Umpire Paul Pryor

Paul Pryor right on top the play! St. Louis vs. Pittsburgh

Paul Pryor makes the call! St. Louis vs. Pittsburgh

Another great call by Paul Pryor in a game at Montreal's Jarry Park

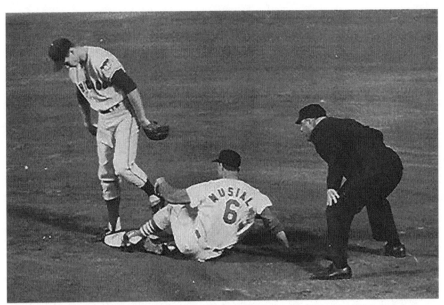

Paul Pryor on the call in a game Cardinals vs. Cubs in St. Louis

Paul Pryor

High School coach Paul Pryor in North Carolina in the 1950's

Big Pops, Paul Pryor

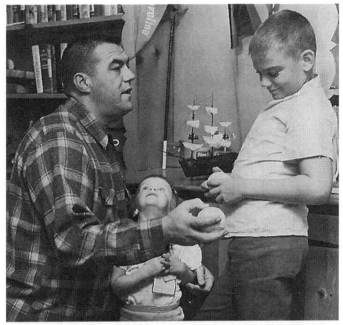

"Big Pops" Paul Pryor at home with children, Paula Ross and Fred

Safe! Great call by Paul Pryor! Home

CHAPTER FIVE

UMPIRES I HAVE KNOWN

"Paul Pryor always seems to be there with a helping hand. I don't think he has an enemy in the world."- Former umpire Frank Schnoorbusch

Umpires travel from city to city in their four man crews. This is not only a protective policy for their own self-defense (the old philosophy that strength is found in numbers), but it is an expedient means of moving together to the hectic schedule of cities.

Each umpire is delegated a certain task to help efficiently move the ensemble. One guy will make the air reservations to the next city season's itinerary. Another umpire arranges the hotel accommodations for the next game. One contacts the overnight air rail express delivery service to make sure the equipment is forwarded to the next park. And the fourth guy, well, he just supervises. That means he is free from doing anything for the time being. He can have a cold one and just enjoy the ride.

The next day's activities are determined by several pending factors. The time of arrival in the new city, the time it takes to settle into the hotel, and the game time all determine what sorts of activities are on the umpire's social agenda. Hypothetically, if we arrived at ten AM in the new town, and the game was at night, we could settle in to the hotel rooms and play nine or eighteen holes of golf. Usually the man assigned the plate duty for that night would call it quits at the ninth hole and relax for the balance of the day. Calling balls and strikes that day always put an umpire on a kind of probationary footing. The eyes and ears of the baseball world are glued to the home plate umpires' calls. You can't afford to be punchy from the sun and exasperated from too many birdies to perform well. The second day in town usually affords a lot more time for extracurricular activities. The last day in town is usually the bummer. All the rigmarole of packing the bags and making the necessary arrangements for the next city and the next game all over again.

While a lot of the guys favored golf or taking in some of the local color of the city, I enjoyed watching the Boob Tube. I was a very, very big TV man. I remember many times when the rest of the umpiring crew would be filing down the hotel hallway with their golf bags and they'd hear me giggling in front of the television. I loved "I Love Lucy" and "Gilligan's Island." Lucy and Ricky Ricardo, Fred and Ethel Mertz, Gilligan, "The Professor," Ginger, Marianne, and Mr. and Mrs. Howell provided hours of stimulating entertainment on road trips.

Umpiring a series in Los Angeles was always a special treat for me. One of the local stations ran an all-night movie fest sponsored by Cal Worthington, one of the nation's leading Ford dealers. I was a real sucker for the oldies-but-goodies. I could finish watching an old John Gardner movie and be all ready to fall asleep when the station would announce an old Bogey flick that I had seen only seventy-one times before. I couldn't fall asleep with that kind of action on the tube.

Umpires in both the American and National League log in excess of 120,000 miles a season. Probably only airline pilots, flight attendants, the Secretary of state, and a few species of migratory birds actually accumulate more flying time than umpires. Because a major league umpire's 120,000 mile plus season involves only six months of the year, this translates to over 20,000 miles per playing month.

There are some differences in the way the two weeks arrange their umpires' itineraries. American Leaguers are nominally on a routine that includes a team's entire homestretch. If the Yankees, for example, are home for a seven-game stint that includes the Red Sox for four games and the Orioles for three, the umpiring crew will be working in Yankee Stadium for both back-to-back series. They'll remain in town for the duration of the Yankee homestretch and then shuffle off to the next home series in another American League park.

The National League travel routine is a little more complex. Umpires are not scheduled to remain in the city for the duration of the team's home stint, but officiate only one series. If the Dodgers are slated to be in Chavez Ravine for seven games to host the Cardinals for the first four and the Giants for the last three games, an umpiring crew will remain in Los Angeles for only one of the two series. While our American League counterparts could roost in a city for up to a week, we were on a more rigorous itinerary that included four days in one city, three in another, and four in yet another.

For six months out of every year, umpires perform the grand process of following the schedule of the National Pastime. All the half-years of an umpiring career can be regarded, in hindsight, in two parts. First and foremost is the actual working time in the stadiums. These several hours on the baseball diamonds each day are their reasons to be, the net result of their traveling, waiting in the airport terminals, accepting the gruff of players and fans, missing their loved ones and the special moments with growing families.

The other side of each year's six-month escapade is the on-the-road life. This is the grand assortment of restaurants, meals, hotel rooms, airports, taxis, golfing, and sharing the camaraderie of crewmates. For nearly every unusual event on the playing field, there seems to be a corresponding tale in the season's schedule chase. The recollections of an umpiring career may include World Series, All-Star games, record breaking occasions, and special moments with special players, but no one could forget the multitude of road stories that seems every bit the part of a career as the shining moments in major league ballparks.

The fellowship shared between four umpires hundreds of miles away from home is a priceless community. The circumstances of traveling so far, so often from home tends to bind umpires together like conspirators. Many of the road stories I remember most vividly seem to involve unusual moments all four crewmembers experience together.

Following the first two games of the 1967 World Series in Boston, the umpires were invited to fly back to St. Louis for the next three on a chartered jet with all the baseball owners and general managers from both leagues. Augie Donatelli and I were part of the National League's umpiring delegation. Excluding postseason games, I had been in the major leagues exactly six seasons and seventeen games. I broke into the majors as the fourth man in the same crew with Augie. I knew him from the first day of my major league career in September 1961, and by 1967, he was still very much an old friend and a great pal, a great umpire, a great family man, and someone who would had taken the extra time to show a rookie umpire some of the inside tricks of the trade.

Augie's the kind of guy you can dress-up, but you can't travel with anywhere. On the playing field, he can make in decisive, brilliant calls, with the calm and collection of an official working a game between two squads of angels. But put him on a plane, taxi, or private car, and it's all over but the tears. Augie is a victim of the Don Knotts Syndrome.

He wanted so desperately to get to his final destination on a common carrier, he harangues a driver or pilot to no end. Stop for a common red light in the car and he wants to know why in the hell you're stopping. His mind accelerates events to the point that he anticipates being at a final destination in his imagination and he can't understand why the plane or taxi hasn't arrived there yet.

The chartered jet carrying baseball's hierarchy arrived in St. Louis and an awaiting bus conveyed all the passengers to their respective hotels in the city. As we were making this grand, imperial sojourn through the Gateway City, I took in the sights while Augie endured a horrendous case of the screaming mee-mees. Augie couldn't understand why the bus was making hotel stops and depositing the assorted mugwumps of baseball. We both had reservations at the Sheraton-Jefferson Hotel, but Augie couldn't understand why the owners had to be dropped off before him.

He was constantly pestering the driver with some less than subtle jibes like, "Come on, bussy, let's go! We're staying at the Sheraton-Jefferson. Come on now, let's go! Let's go, bussy!" Augie could drive a strong man to drink on road trips.

During World War II, he served in the Army Air Corps and was captured by the Nazis. How the Germans ever managed to contain him in one stalag is almost beyond imagination. No one has ever determined whether the period of detainment changed Augie. Some people think he was so bent on reaching a final destination that he was celebrating V-E Day in his own mind long before the war was over.

"Pope Paul" Owens of the Phillies and Mayo Smith of the Phils happen to be on the same charter flight and bus trip in St. Louis as Augie and me. If they had felonious bone in their bodies and they had to listen to one more "Hey, hey, hey, bussy!," Augie would have been shot.

Former Phils manager Mayo Smith couldn't hold back any longer. Someone had to say something to Augie or knock him out, there was nothing in between. I knew Augie was outrageous to travel with and chalked-up the episode as still another road adventure. This was par for the course, those who didn't know him were apt to think he had just taken flight from his senses.

Mayo Smith had heard enough and just couldn't resist giving Augie the business. "Hey, Augie," he called out in the bus, "how'd they ever keep you in a prison camp anyways?"

"It wasn't easy," Augie replied. The entire bus broke out in a roar of laughter.

A cab driver in New York City did something to Augie that crossed my mind a number of times. The great Jocko Conlan and Augie Donatelli had just finished umpiring a Brooklyn Dodgers game in Ebbets Field. Both umpires left the game together and boarded a taxi on Bedford Avenue for Manhattan. Augie was in a desperate backseat driving mood and drove the hackie to the brink of insanity. The taxi driver was so infuriated by Augie's questions of why he should stop at red lights, when he wasn't in Manhattan already, when he took this route instead of that one, he decided to set his loud-mouthed passenger straight once and for all. He stopped his cab on the Brooklyn Bridge and dropped Jocko and Augie off midway between the spans. It was an awfully long hike back to Broadway – especially for Jocko Conlan.

But Augie never changed. Both of us finished umpiring a Braves game in Milwaukee in 1964. I happen to be the umpire out of the four man crew responsible for making air reservations. We had to be in Los Angeles the next day and North Central Airlines was the only carrier at the time that flew from Milwaukee to O'Hare in Chicago and then on to Los Angeles. The umpiring detachment arrived at the Milwaukee Airport with four first-class reservations to face the next day's game at Dodgers Stadium.

We were ready for the North Central flight to Chicago, but the jet wasn't ready for us. Mechanical complications were making in a timely crease in our schedule. This was unfathomable to Augie. By astral projection, he was already camped out in a hotel room in Los Angeles. A plane unable to expeditiously conveying him to his destination was as outrageous as a game without bats and balls – it just didn't happen. Augie went nuts at the news that the North Central flight couldn't take off for O'Hare. He began a long, long, one-man campaign against the airlines. North Central Airlines were a bunch of bums as far as he was concerned. He swore he never would board another one of their planes, anywhere, anyhow. Just looking at the silver bird under repair infuriated him. The damned plane was right in front of him he couldn't board it! Then a terrible thought crossed Augie's mind. He was utterly convinced we would have to drive to Chicago in order to pick-up a Los Angeles bound flight. God forbid! This notion was as loathsome to Augie as facing the devil eyeball to eyeball.

Augie ranted and raved about having to drive to O'Hare and was so discombobulated about the situation that he threw an empty beer can at the sickly jet. In the end, North Central got the plane in proper operating condition and we took off like real champs to Chicago and then to Los Angeles International. But Augie was so frustrated about the situation that he had double vision all the way to the West Coast.

Augie lives near me in Florida and we see a lot of one another. There is always a charity, or a fantasy camp or an old-timers' game that bring us together. On November 16 and 17, 1985, Augie and I were asked to umpire an old-timers' game in Orlando. A star-studded cast of managers, Hall of Famer's, and great names from the past were scheduled to take part in the game.

I drove my blue Chevy van I use for my sports luggage business to Orlando with Augie in the passenger's seat and a group of young, minor-league umpires in the back. Augie was on unfairly good behavior until we reached the stadium.

Evidently we were early to the ballpark and no one had arranged a brass greeting party for us. We were locked out of the designated parking area for the game's participants. I honked the horn a few times, but none of the attendants seem to be around. Augie interpreted this is a bad omen.

"Ooooooh, nnnnnnnoooooo, they locked us out!," he shouted. "We won't be able to get in!! Were locked out!! Oh, Christ, here we go!!!

This was nothing especially new to me, but the minor league guys seem to think a catastrophe had just occurred. They looked at each other with expressions that reflected both surprise and horror.

Oh, nnnoooooo, we're locked out! That's it!! They locked us out!!! Augie kept yelling.

I delicately explained to the umpires how Augie gets a "little" nervous on road trips and drove the van into another parking area that was open.

Eddie Vargo was another umpire with nerves of steel on the field but subject to frequent attacks of the heebe-jeebees out of the ballpark. Eddie was not crazy about flying. Period. There were times when he would have rather crawled bare-knuckled to the next city than face a jet ride.

If we had to leave for the airport after a game, Eddie was usually studying the skies in the late innings. He became more adept at recognizing cloud covers and thunder banks than Willard Scott. Occasionally, one of the umpires would walk up to Eddie as he was perusing the heavens and give him a little pep talk. "Ooooohhh boy, are we ever going to have a rocky ride. Just look at those thunderheads rolling in, Eddie." He'd timidly glanced at the sky while his face lost all color. He looked like he just received news that he was to be shot at sunrise.

Once we left a stadium to catch a shuttle flight to Philadelphia for a game the next day. Eddie had a severe case of meteorological misgivings and decided the skies were too gruesome for planes. While we made the jaunt to the airport, Eddie made arrangements to take a train to Philadelphia. It was only one hundred miles between New York and the City of Brotherly Love, and Eddie decided he'd rather be safe than sorry.

Bill Jackowski, another member of the crew, had a friend in Haddonfield, New Jersey who owned the Monticello Motor Lodge there. Frequently, when we were in the Philadelphia area to work a game at Veterans Stadium, the crew would stay at the Monticello. It was a short ride from the city and afforded the crew a rare opportunity to spend a night or two in exurbia.

The rest of the crew arrived in Haddonfield while Eddie's train was still chugging along the tracks. But we prepared a festive celebration for Eddie's arrival. When he finally drove into the Monticello Lodge, we had the marquee program appropriately decorated –WELCOME NERVES VARGO. Oh, we were bad.

"On the road" for me meant not only chasing the 162 game seasonal schedule, but making speaking engagements during the off-season. From 1964, I was hired by the Schaefer Circle of Sports to represent the brewery at all sorts of social and sporting events. Most of the time, Circle members went in pairs to any speaking function. Jerry Philbin of the New York Jets, pitcher Jim Bouton, and Mark Belanger of the Baltimore Orioles were frequently my partners on the rubber chicken circuit.

Fans and curiosity seekers always had mixed feelings when a ballplayer and an umpire appeared publicly for a pas de deux. One category of fans looked at us dumbfounded as if the presence of an ump and a ball player together was an incongruous combination. We were supposed to be natural enemies on and off the field. If we weren't screaming in each other's faces like we were supposed to, any other public appearance seem to be false staging. Another category of sports aficionados ogled at the player, asked a few baseball questions, requested an autograph and then eyeballed me suspiciously. Not many people had ever been face to face with an umpire before and their looks and conversation usually reflected their ambivalence. As far as most fans are concerned, umpires are a generic species of officials. They are the guys who only get cameo roles on the televised game and make the camera close-ups when a player or manager is bawling them out. One umpire basically looks, dresses, and acts like all the other umpires. When the Schaefer Circle of Sports afforded me the chance to be examined at close range, the fans took every opportunity to scrutinize this unusual species of humanity with a jeweler's eye. I felt like a rare, new addition to a zoo's collection. Only the very, very best of fans could distinguish us from the ballpark programs.

After umpires became thoroughly versed as practitioners and enforcers of the rule book, they usually liked to toy with adaptations in style. The logic behind this is simple. Despite the opinion of the few umpire-hams in the trade, fans pay good money at the turnstiles to see the players in action. Umpires are the necessary footnotes to the sport. They wear the same blue, nondescript uniforms without embroidered names or numbers like the players and outside some of the more obvious differences in height and girth, they tend to look like one another on the field. An individual style differentiates one umpire from his fellow tradesmen. It is his trademark, his unique fingerprint on the game.

Umpires in the minors who someday want big league duty adopt a style to be noticed by major league officials. In a game that is played with a body of standard rules and officiated by umpires in standard uniforms, an individual style is a small, creative leeway that sets one umpire apart from all others.

Most guys cultivate a comfortable style of their own in the minors. By the time they reach the majors, they've been practicing their own gyrations for years. But there is another school of umpires, however, who feel they should be a sideshow to the main attraction of the game. These guys are the oppressed hams wrapped in blue umpires' limits. They take the small creative aspects and develop them into a nightclub routine. They perform carefully choreographed antics in hopes of standing out on television. They pirouette and genuflect to the beat of safes and outs on the field. When some irate managers perform a primitive fertility dance in their frustrations, these guys tend to augment the heat of the moment by responding with their own dance numbers.

I raised my fists a la John L. Sullivan to indicate a strike. It felt comfortable and seemed emphatic enough, although some players unfamiliar with me assumed I was prepared to box their ears. Chris Pelakoudas made the Greek sign of the cross to indicate a strike. That was a nice touch, it gave a little ecclesiastical feeling to the game. Augie Donatelli had a kind of cavalier stance of calling balls and strikes on one knee. The late Tony Venson was a practitioner of the silent but deadly treatment. When Tony made a call on the bases, he pointed sternly at the base. The runners always seemed to know when they were safe for out on one of Tony's calls, but no one else did. Once he called a close play on the bases and drew a laser-powered finger at the base. The late Bob Prince of KDKA radio said that he couldn't tell if Tony was indicating whether the player was safe or out. "I guess will have to watch if the runner leaves the base to see if he's out," he told his listening audience.

Most umpires are not built like Rudolph Nureyev, (John McSherry, Kenny Kaiser, and I are testimony to that), but there are some who like to pirouette in the air and land before they make a call on the base paths. I was just too big to be a leaper. I could probably have jumped high enough, but I would have injured myself on the reentry into the Earth's atmosphere.

There are all sorts of subtle moves umpires adopt to separate themselves from the dozens of drab men in blue suits. Ron Luciano used to point his finger at a guy with his finger cocked like a trigger and shoot 'em down. In a staccato voice, he'd shout," Outoutoutoutoutout!" and blow 'em away in their tracks. Dutch Rennert is a great umpire but at times he can go through more gyrations than Gene Kelly when he calls a man out. But the majority of umpires are not flamboyant enough to be recognized from the common garden variety on the field.

Following virtually any speaking engagement, there are certain questions I can always anticipate being asked. People are fascinated by the fact that I spent twenty years in the majors. Whether they are amazed that someone could be so foolhardy to be a gluten for abuse for so long, or whether they're astonished that someone could work in a profession all those years without any respect, I don't know. But one of the most frequently asked questions I encounter involve general comparisons between the caliber of ballplayers in 1961, when I reached the majors, and those in 1982, the year I retired.

The objectives, fundamentals, and overall play of baseball has not really changed during the course of my two decades in the big leagues. Players are still human beings with their own talents, pride, and even their own mean axes to grind. Pitchers still throw the ball the same distance from the mound to home plate with the same objectives in mind. A bunt entails running the same, long 90 feet to a haven on per space, a stolen second base involves traversing the same ninety feet worth of real estate – although now it is sometimes over Astroturf instead of good ole infield dirt. But there is a vast difference in the general fabric between players in 1961 and 1982.

During my 20 years in the majors, I would sometimes give casual off-the-field advice to a promising young player that gave 100% on the field. In 1962, I could tell a pitcher like Jim Maloney of the Mets that he should concentrate more on the mound and take his time between pitches. Just by closely observing a pitcher, I could detect when he sometimes felt rushed and had the tendency to lose concentration. I never was the kind of umpire to buttonhole a player out of the ballpark and perform my own one-man instructional league, but for a few young players that had the goods to become big stars, I would give an occasional tidbit of advice.

In the early 60s, a player was apt to listen to this sort of critique with interest and gratitude. Criticism had not yet become anathema. Any suggestion that could be translated into a better performance was cordially accepted. More than infrequently they would respond with, "Thanks, Mr. Pryor, I think you're right. Next time I'll try to remember that on the field."

The players of 1982, as a whole, were prima donnas. If you gave a promising young player thirty seconds of advice passing through a hotel lobby, an umpire is likely to get a call from a manager very soon. "Say, you have a hard enough time umpiring. Are you a coach now?" Another popular one is, "What are you trying to do? Are you playing coach now, Pryor?" If Warren Spahn was eager to listen to any suggestions that might help his performances – what makes a 20-year-old hurler in the 1980s so uppity?

In general, players did not look upon themselves in 1961 as big ticket commodities in a big ticket sport with contract attorneys, agents, commercials, and blue chip stocks. Many players today are only willing to accept advice from their two best friends, Dow Jones and Ginnie Mae. If the great baseball writer, Ring Lardner, was still typing, he'd have to take a stockbrokers' course just to understand the new dimensions of the game.

None of my after-dinner speeches has ever been a carbon copy of another. Most of the time, I wasn't even sure of what I'd say until a few minutes before my trip to the rostrum. Thirty years as an umpire gave me enough riotous stories to keep any kind of audience entertained. If a player or manager happened to be in the National League long enough to be assigned a locker, chances were good that I had a comical story about him. I could tell gas house stories to a bunch of drunken varmints or boys' life tales depicting a player's diligence and hard work to Little Leaguers. Sometimes, I even experimented with a few concoctions on my own. I thought it would be fun to dissect the word "umpire" into its individual letters and lists the appropriate professional attributes for each letter. The one word meaning that corresponded to each letter has never changed, but the explanation I've given always seemed to change.

U – U is for understanding. A good umpire not only understands the rules that govern baseball, but understands the rules of the field and the players in the game.

M – M is for modesty. Nobody pays, or, I should say nobody in their right mind, pays good money to see Paul Pryor or John McSherry or Augie Donatelli run around the field calling safes and outs. Umpires are the technical moderators of the game, not the playing stars. Once, at a sports banquet in Rockford, Illinois, in 1974, a sportswriter approached me and asked, "So you're Paul Pryor? You've been in the National League for 12 years, right? Well, I've never heard of you before."

I told him "thanks for the compliment," and I really meant it. Umpire should only be seen and heard in their own specific context of the game.

P – P is for patience. Listen to the players, acknowledge their supermarket of beefs, but be sure of yourself. A good umpire makes one call and one call only. Ultimately, umpires and doctors function the same way, you've got to have the patience to continue the profession.

I – I is for being impartial. Contrary to popular opinion, umpires are not hired by teams, but by a league. They are responsible to the game of baseball and work for the league, not individual teams. The owners appropriate a certain amount of money to the leagues at the beginning of each season that pays for the umpires' salary and expenses. Fines levied on ballplayers bypass the wallets and find their way into the war chests of each league.

R – R is very simple – umpires are Right all the time. I leave this one alone.

E – E is for Emphatic. If an umpire is not emphatic, then players, managers and even the fans have the tendency not to believe you. Umpire needs to let the whole world know his call on a plate.

My first opportunity to make a solo appearance before a large audience occurred in 1967. The Schaefer Circle of Sports must have been either crazy or had extraordinary confidence in me because I was dispatched to address the New York Traffic Club. These are the big wheels in Brooks' Brothers suits and diamond stick pins who run and own the Big Apple. There were close to 200 at the gathering and it took only a few minutes for me to realize that this was not going to be like speaking before the Northern South Dakota Prairie League softball beer bash.

During the cocktail hour that preceded the luncheon, one of the members responsible for the club's festivities took me aside for a quick pep talk. He told me that the last sports personality to address the Traffic Club was the former middleweight boxing champion, Rocky Graziano. I smiled to myself. At least they weren't expecting someone who spoke to King's American like William F Buckley, Jr. Or anyone who was going to deliver an esoteric lecture on the kinesiological wonders of professional baseball players.

"I hope you're not as vulgar as he was," the Traffic Club man cautioned me.

"The worst thing I say at a meeting like this is 'damn,'" I told him. He obviously knew nothing about umpires because he would have thrown me out right then and there for that reply.

"Everything with that man was 'f' this and 'f' that," he said. After I reassured him that this would not be the case with me, he stopped shaking and sweating.

I had no prepared speech simply because baseball had given me ready anecdotes for several full lifetimes. But this was not exactly a collection of meat and potatoes guys who walk around with gravy stains on their flapping shirttails. These were the grand mullahs of New York business and I realized I'd have to treat them a little differently.

As I surveyed the audience from the dais, I noticed that most of the men were paying little or no attention to anyone at the rostrum. The speaker was awarding ten and fifteen year membership pins, but no one seemed to give a damn. Guys were chit-chatting and leaving their seats to mingle with their buddies at a distant table. I decided that no matter what I said, I would get their undivided attention. I somehow knew that tucked deep inside their $800 suits, worked the hearts of some real hell-raisers.

After the Traffic Club emcee introduced me, I approached the rostrum to the accompaniment of a polite round of applause. I was determined to change that immediately.

"Who in the hell are you kidding?" I bellowed. Guys involved in their private conversations all over the dining room lifted their heads. "No one claps for an umpire," I shouted. "You've got to boo me!!"

A series of funny, reserved Bronx cheers erupted throughout the room. I kept shouting and raising my hand in encouragement. The shouting increased as the entire New York Traffic Club pounded their fists in boos. I knew was going to have fun with this. Behind their horn-rimmed glasses lurked the same sensibilities as the beer night fans.

Once I got them going, I found it hard to keep them quiet long enough to speak. I had to shout, "Take a seventh inning stretch!" to reach enough peace and quiet. But once the noise dwindled to a subtler roar, I picked out certain tables and gave them a lesson in some real umpire talk. "Hey, table number 62 – shut up or I'll run you out like a big-mouthed manager!" They loved it. No one addressed them like this since they were scolded by their governesses when they were six years old.

I told them that my parish was the only one I knew that ever had bucket seats. It had a drive-in confessional. When the Bishop found out about what was going on he demanded that the priest explain this strange activity. The priest informed him that the "toot n' tell or go to hell" philosophy is causing a nice traffic jam.

For some reason, this corny joke just popped into my head. But that Traffic Club loved it. I could have handed out party favors and funny hats and they would have as easily gone along with that.

I dissected the word U-M-P-I-R-E and they loved that routine. In fact, the response was even a little scary. With all the assembled money magnets and tycoons in the palm of my hand, I was in the position to lead the second Industrial Revolution. I could have had them march down Wall Street shouting and screaming anything that came into my head, in between blowing imaginary trombones. I knew then how Robespierre must've felt before the excited masses.

The Traffic Club had seated me on the dais next to a guy I thought was a dentist. Somehow our dinner conversation revolved around teeth – missing teeth, chipped teeth, bridgework, caps, broken jaws, as well as my professional hazards of balls and bats careening into mouths. My new friend seemed to be thoroughly versed in dental anatomy. I promised to look him up in the city the next time I happened to be bounced in the mouth at Shea Stadium. He assured me that he'd take good, professional care for me.

At the close of my speech, I thanked the gentlemen of the club for their attention, thanked Schaefer Beer for such a great audience and extended my thanks to the emcee for seating me besides the good dentist. Then someone informed me while I was still at the speaker's rostrum that my cordial neighbor was not a dentist at all, but the local mortician. I looked over at the guy on the dais in shock and then said, "I don't know why my teeth are shattering so much, but I'll have to sit down now!"

Usually only one member of the Circle of Sports was dispatched to any single speaking engagement. But Schaefer made a clear distinction between umpires and players when it came to paychecks. Umpires receive hundred $150 per festivity plus expenses while players received $250 per event plus expenses. Actually, I considered this a form of highway robbery because I was wined and dined and had the chance to be a ham in the dais spotlights. I felt like I was in heaven for most of the speaking engagements but many of the players acted like they had just been condemned to hell. The idea of $250 plus expenses was just not enough for them to mingle with the likes of commoners.

I was with Mark Belanger of the Baltimore Orioles at a sports function. I gave my 20 minute foray on umpiring in the majors, told a few Casey Stengel stories and returned to my seat. Mark followed me in the speakers' rotation and proceeded to list the Orioles' roster. He suggested that the young, aspiring ballplayers in the audience give their 100% effort on and off the field, work hard at fielding and hitting and then sat down. His entire speech may have lasted two and a half minutes. He might as well have cut the formalities and asked the audience point blank – my expenses came to this amount, and I am entitled to $250 – who do I see about this, and will this be in the form of check or cash?

This problem with the Schaefer athletes was only symptomatic of the greater changes among the major league players in the early and mid-Sixties. There seemed to be a polemical relationship that was developing then between money and all other matters excluding money. While contracts, contract attorneys, bonuses, and Mercedes began to consume their energies – the other responsibilities to baseball, to the fans, and to the community were on the wane. Their individual and collective profiles within the sport were rapidly changing. No payment seem to justify their growing self-worth. The image they had collectively created for themselves was rapidly exceeding the image that fans across the country perceived. Hence, $250 was no longer a viable amount of money for a baseball player to spend two hours at a sports function.

Most of the time, umpires are only recognized in public when they are wearing a name card or sandwich board with their names emblazoned on it, and even then, nobody really seems to care. For good reasons, fans flock to players and usually circle an umpire cautiously a few times at any event before they dare speak to him. This can have sad psychological repercussions for any umpire who is a born ham.

Shortly after the 1980 World Series, I went to Manchester, New Hampshire, to speak at a dinner. I shared the podium in the city armory with such baseball greats as Ted Williams, Tony Perez, Steve Stone, Vida Blue, and Jim Palmer. When the autograph session began, the players were inundated by an onslaught of fans seeking their signatures on napkins, flyers, virtually anything that retained ink. I signed my name a grand total of six times. Only a few days earlier, I had been working the World Championship between the Phillies and the Royals. Even though I had just addressed the audience on umpiring the World Series, no one seemed particularly enthusiastic about knowing much more about me or the games. I twiddled my thumbs and chatted with a few die-hards while the mob surrounded the players.

Ted Williams realized this and felt a little sorry for me. I was in the men's room when he escaped the masses long enough to take a breather from the reams of paper accumulating around him. He knew he'd be writing his name for hours.

"Paul, why don't you sign some of these autographs?" he asked.

"Not in this life as an umpire," I thought to myself. I had to decline. The fans wanted to meet and get the signature of the great Ted Williams. Walking home with Paul Pryor etched on a table napkin would have made the whole evening seem anti-climactic for most fans.

During most of my career in the big leagues, Racine, Wisconsin was home for me and my growing family. Instead of remaining in North Carolina on the East Coast, Racine was only half a continent flight from the eastern and western extremities of the National League. During any hiatus of a few days in my umpiring schedule, I would fly to Wisconsin to be with my family and then resume the season's chase for the next game in the next Stadium.

Umpiring in the major leagues was sufficient credentials for celebrityhood in Racine. I was frequently called upon by St. Lucy's parish there to organize charity benefits. Depending on the timing of my schedule, I could parade back to Racine with a group of ballplayers for a charity banquet of one kind or another.

Once in 1964, I organized a benefit at St. Lucy's and invited a number of baseball and football players and a few fellow umpires to share the dais and entertain the audience with some toastmaster humor. I invited my old buddy and fellow pundit Bob Uecker to deliver a few words of his baseball wisdom. Bob was late when the banquet seating began, but he managed to arrive during salad time without looking too obvious.

As master of ceremonies, I introduced each sports guest and turned the microphone over to them to entertain the parishioners. When I introduced Uecker to the audience, he rose hesitantly from his seat and walked over to grab the microphone from me. He apologized for being unable to speak at the moment because he had to go to the bathroom.

The good nuns in the front tables nearly swallowed their desserts whole. Bob returned to the microphone to me and began walking off the dais in search of the men's room. The audience was totally stunned. Bob had not yet reached his Lite Beer fame and only the true fans in the seats knew him to be a practical joker.

When he realized that the entire reception hall believed he was making an honest walk to the john, he turned around, walked to the microphone and informed everyone that he was just joking. He apologized for being late to St. Lucy's and claimed his delay was unavoidable. A small fire had started in his bathroom and he was forced to stick around because he was worried it might travel all the way through his backyard to his home.

In 1968, I returned to Woonsocket, Rhode Island, for my first hometown speaking engagement. Since I joined the Schaefer Circle of Sports in 1964, the banquet circuits had almost become an off-season vocation and avocation for me. Sometimes I would be at as many as three separate functions a day in a metropolitan area. Breakfast might be with a Lions Club, lunch could bring me to a Sons of Italy feast, and dinner might entail a B'nai Brith banquet. By the time spring training arrived again, Weight Watchers clubs across the country were soliciting my lifetime membership dues.

Sharing the dais at a function in Cincinnati, or Buffalo, or New York City, or any of the other cities Schaefer sent me to, meant addressing audiences I knew little or nothing about and vice versa. Speaking before a club in Woonsocket meant facing people who knew me. The old cliché, "You can't go home again," ran through my mind time and again in route to Rhode Island. It wasn't so much the notion that "familiarity breeds contempt" that bothered me, it was just the idea that familiarity meant I couldn't tell lies. THESE GUYS KNEW ME. Even the culprit who perpetrated the de-pansing incident might have been in the audience chuckling to himself. There would be people at the gathering who knew things about me that I didn't even know.

The Striped Bass Fishing Club of Woonsocket invited me through Schaefer to address their organization at Vermette's Diner. This was a big event for the city. For some strange reason, I expected the local newspapers to embrace by visit with a story-heading like, "Local Boy Returns from Major League Baseball to a Warm Hometown Greeting." Instead, my arrival was announced with the appointment question – "What does Paul Pryor know about fishing?"

It was a memorable occasion for me because the tables were finally turned at Vermette's. Instead of walking in to order a hot turkey sandwich with mashed potatoes and gravy, I was the distinguished speaker.

I met a lot of old friends and told a number of funny baseball stories, but my last line unintentionally seemed to draw the most laughs. In closing, I made the mistake of saying, "I'd like to congratulate the Striped *Ass* Fishing Club for winning their tournament." I felt so small I could have sat on home plate and dangled my legs. My old friends laughed as they shook their heads in disbelief. I had no problem reading their minds – you can dress a guy up and send them off to the majors, but when he returns home again, he's in the same shape you left him! Home

CHAPTER SIX

MANAGERS

"There's nothing like umpiring in the major leagues. It's hard work, because during a game you have to bear down every second. It's the kind of life I've always dreamed about. We stay in the best hotels, travel in the fast planes, and there's never a dull moment." –Paul Pryor

Contrary to popular opinion, the organist is not the loneliest person in a major league stadium. Managers are either the desolation angels or solitary bums of the franchise. They are held accountable by team owners and fans for the balance sheet of wins and losses. Their euphoria or desperation on and off the field is usually linked to their position in the division standings. The failure of the bullpen during the course of the season, the inability of last year's sluggers to translate their prowess into hits, even the poor second base arm of a catcher are ultimately blamed on the manager. As field commander of the 25 man brigade delegated to battle 162 times a season, he is a reaper of the attendance harvest, arbitrator of division standings, and steward of things that are and things soon to come in the destiny of his team.

Apart from players, the umpires and managers in the sport know the inherent hazards of the job when they sign a big league contract. Umpires know they will be abused by players and fans on the field. Managers know that the placard above their locker space is only inviolable as long as the team's autocracy is willing to accept the bottom line statistics he has accumulated. Baseball naturally endows managers and umpires with conflicting purposes. Umpires are nominally delegated to enforce the law of the Rule Book, and occasionally involve themselves in arbitration on the field. As helmsman of a baseball team, managers will seek to give their players as much freedom of performance they can without breaking the rules. Umpires are guardians of the status quo, managers operate on the terrain owned by the Rules, but they scour it for any items that might gain them any extra advantage. They sit in the dugouts and scout the perimeters by the barbed wire in search of the right opportunity to bring out their giant shears undetected. In the clear terms of "Hogan's Heroes," umpires are like the Colonel Klinks of the sport while the managers have more the artful dodger mentality of a Colonel Hogan. Usually the motives between the two cross wires and spark when they shout in each others' faces at close range on the field.

There are more synonyms for a baseball manager then in an entire thesaurus. Besides the obvious job description of orchestrating a team on the field, managers are chaplains, psychologists, master judges of athletic talent, soothsayers, purveyors of 20/20 hindsight, team moderators, arbitrators, assistants in labor negotiations, probation officers, delinquent officers, personnel managers, decision-makers during climactic situations, and press secretaries – just to name a few.

I've always thought that the primary measure of a good manager was his ability to take the team and make the very most of its talent potential. A star manager could examine the individual facets of each player and compose a roster that will, at least, become contenders. Pennant and World Series managers are not automatically included in this select group. Theoretically, a manager could acquire a squad similar to the 1949 Yankees and reach Golconda without much effort. Talent abounded out of their pinstripes. Each man's skills nicely encountered his natural talents. But taking a last place team with marginal talent and finishing in third place in the division – as a contender – is a managerial accomplishment.

No two umpires in the same league seem to share the same opinion of a manager. Some umpires have had feuds with managers while they were both in the minors that carry over into their big league careers. Even men on the same officiating crew can have conflicting feelings about a team skipper. The manager can recite the Riot Act line by line to one umpire and treat the other three men in the crew like gods. It depends upon the chemistry between their personalities and any call on the field that might cause bad feelings.

An important point I tried to impress on rookies was never to let a veteran umpire pass his enemies down to them. When I was first in the majors, one of the old timers took me aside and read off a laundry list of reasons why Cincinnati Reds' manager Fred Hutchinson was a no good so-and-so. He was one of the people umpires had to be on guard for. I was supposed to watch my P's and Q's around Hutchinson because he liked to have a "private" relationship with umpires. He was like a Marine Corps drill sergeant and the umpires were the buck privates.

Fred turned out to be a real nice guy. I didn't even have to kick him out of games that often. But I quickly learned that a greenhorn umpire should not inherit another veteran's old battle sores. An exception to this practical rule, of course, are inveterate wisenheimers like Leo Durocher, Billy Martin, and Earl Weaver – that's a completely different story.

The worst possible situation for an umpire is to feel intimidated by a manager on the field. This usually only happens to the less experienced umpires. Some guys who have had a nasty brush with a manager may have the entire incident flash before their eyes the split second before they call a close play. They envision the manager charging out on the diamond like a Gurhka warrior for another round of battle with them. The young umpire may give his team the benefit of the doubt in a photo finish play. Sometimes a veteran umpire can sense this and he'll continued to browbeat a greenhorn in the hopes that intimidation will pay off. Leo "The Lip" Durocher was a practitioner of this philosophy.

A manager may sometimes operate under the opinion that an umpire is "on his side." This is a potentially dangerous situation. They may have a friendly history on the field or several close plays may have been called in the manager's favor even if he privately knew his man was probably out. He assumes that the umpire may secretly be a rooter for his team. But as soon as an unfavorable call is made, the manager is crushed. He'll run onto the field with an expression that does not so much connote the belief that his man was legitimately safe, but wears a look that unmistakably communicates betrayal. "How could you!! How could you of all umpires do this to me!!

Veteran umpires and managers usually shed these little idiosyncrasies with time. Each close play is made on a clean slate. Hence, the umpire makes an honest call without fear or favor and the manager disagrees with it because any umpire is invariably a horse's ass out to get him. Now that's real baseball!

Time has a unique way of seasoning baseball people. A young Turk manager may argue a play like an attorney approaching the bench. Things have a way of being very clinical. But a collision between a veteran manager and umpire is more like a friendly argument between two country neighbors. Both are slightly jaded from a life of long bus rides and season after season in the sun. Chances are good that both already know each others' habits and peeves. They may even know each others' families and they have long ago recognized the fact that they're crazy enough to be adults who are paid to work a little boys' game. The most interesting manager moments were with the seasoned veterans. In fact, dealing with Casey Stengel on the field was like a father and his middle-aged son kindly rehashing an old problem.

The early Mets had a short-live tradition of setting aside one day a season to play the Army baseball team from West Point. For those few magic hours, the Black Knights of the Hudson were able to play a big league team. For those few dubious hours, the Mets played a college team and got the opportunity to take a very serious look at themselves in the mirror. Casey Stengel and the Mets had just finished an encounter with the Cadets before they had to return to the real world and face the Philadelphia Phillies. Casey handed me his line-up card at home plate and I made the mistake of taking a few steps away before I actually examined it.

The line-up card looked like a random draft from a strange, out-of-state telephone directory. I scouted the Mets warming-up on the field and had a double take Casey's line-up card. It seemed as though Stengel had done a strange theme and variation between the players causing the ball around the field and the official line-up card. There were Joe Palookas and Fred Palookas on the card that forgot to make it to the game. Evidently, Casey had either invented an ideal line-for a future generation of Mets or I was in a time warp.

Casey had Rod Kanehl in the line-up, but Kanehl wasn't even on the field warming-up. He had designated Choo-Choo Coleman as catcher, but Chris Cannizzaro was receiving the warm-pitches. My next task was to saunter over to the Phillies' dugout and give manager Gene Mauch the good news. But in the long walk in the sun from the home plate area to the Phillies' dugout, I realized Casey made a big mistake. I knew the Mets had just played the West Point Cadets and had the sneaking suspicion that in the midst of his own wisdom, Casey had inadvertently handed me the line-up he devised for the Army game. I didn't know if Gene Mauch would have a sense of humor about the situation, but I quickly found out he didn't. Gene insisted that Stengel had to play with the line-up card he turned in at the pre-game meeting at home plate. He was adamant in this point and threaten to protest the game if this was the case. The logistics of the game were not going to be abridged simply because Casey Stengel happened to turn in the wrong line-up card, period, period, period.

"You can't protest the game," I told Mauch. "It hasn't even started yet."

A temporary band-aide like that was just not good enough Gene Mauch. I was face to face with the notion of having a forfeited game on my hands before a pitch was thrown. Time was running out and a different Met team from the line-up card was enthusiastically warming-up for the game.

I made a quick decision and told Gene that the team on the field was, in effect, the team of the line-up card. Position and place on the field would supersede whatever nonsense Casey Stengel had on his card. This was a horse pill Gene wasn't willing to swallow delicately, but after some hard-nosed convincing on my part, he seemed to finally take it down in one large gulp.

I marched over to the Mets dugout and spoke to Stengel. I handed him back the Joe Palooka line-up card and said, "Casey, rip that S.O.B. card up so you don't get the line-up all screwed up again." He tore the old Army game squad card and slowly produced the right card from his back pocket.

I remember one occasion behind the plate when Casey Stengel had a difficult time selecting a relief Picher. Jay Hook was pitching for the Mets and he ran into a "little trouble" on the mound. This was an ailment that had become quite contagious among the pitching staff of the early Mets. Casey decided to leave his throne in the dugout to have a word with Hook on the mound.

I immediately began my very special manager-pitcher count reserved for these occasions. I would count one one thousand, two one thousand, three one thousand, all the way to nine one thousand and then march to the mound. As they reached the perimeter of the mound and was within earshot of Stengel and Hook, I realized Casey was biding for time and wasn't even talking about baseball.

He resorted to that special lingo managers sometimes used to postpone for time to make a pitching change. Casey was speaking with feeling and gusto about "the tri-form before the turn" and offering new and imaginative suggestions about such subjects as the Birds and the Bees.

"Casey, are you making a pitching change? I asked.

Stengel shook his head and claimed that everything was fine. "No, son, let's just play the game." With that, Casey trotted back to the dugout while I walked back to dust off the plate.

True to form, I correctly positioned my derrière to the mound as I swept off the plate. Umpiring etiquette requires that umpires sweep the plate with their butts pointed to the outfield. It was considered an insult to the fans when the umpire took a bow to sweep the plate and emphasized his backside. This is very understandable, particularly with umpires the size of me, Ron Luciano, Kenny Kaiser, Joe West, and John McSherry. If we bent over for the fans, they wouldn't have to wait any longer before they saw New York.

But as I was bent with my bottom to the mound to sweep the plate, I heard a woman call out loud and clear to the picture, "Throw the ball now and knock his brains out!!" This, on top of Casey's antics was quickly making this an extra-strength aspirin ordeal.

Play had barely resumed again before Casey made another pilgrimage to Hook on the mound. I again began one of my one one thousand… nine one thousand counts and paraded to Stengel and his pitcher.

"Casey, who are you putting in the game?" I asked. He looked at me with a curious expression on his face and said, "I don't know, Pryor. You tell me. You've been guessing all day anyways."

Stengel finally summoned Willard Hunter, a young southpaw, to mound duty and the game continued smoothly. A few weeks later I happened to bump into Casey in the bar at the Netherlands Hilton Hotel in Cincinnati. I couldn't resist mentioning something about his indecisiveness and making that pitching change.

"Casey, you senile old goat. What were you trying to do, cross me up on the field?" I asked.

"Well, Paul, I wasn't sure which team the new pitcher would come from," Casey informed me.

"What do you mean?" I knew Casey was setting me up for a real curveball.

"Well," he said, thinking very deliberately, "We actually have four teams. One team is coming, one team is going, there's one team on the field, and then there's the team in General Manager George Weiss' mind." Insightful words of wisdom.

Whenever a rookie umpire asked me for any general advice, I usually gave him the same tried-and-true logic that was handed down to me in 1961 and 1962. Above all else, just be yourself – do what you did in the minor leagues because that's what elevated you to the majors. But it wouldn't be fair to any rookie to withhold the Leo Durocher Rule. This is part of showing a new umpire the ropes and may prevent him from being hung from one. A rookie umpire is similar to an inexperienced gladiator going into the Coliseum against an experience lion when it came to Leo. He loved to eat them alive.

It is difficult to adequately describe Leo to a young person who has no recollection of what he was like as a manager. You have to sometimes resort to drawing a picture. "Do you know what Earl Weaver is like when he's mad on the field?" I'll ask. Okay. "And do you know how Billy Martin sometimes gets hot under the collar?" Okay. "Well. Leo Durocher was just like that except he's bald."

If a greenhorn umpire happen to be working a game, Durocher usually delivered his fire and brimstone sermon to him. He shouted from the dugout to browbeat the rookie. He ranted and raved about most calls the young umpire made whether they were in his favor or not. Leo just wanted to be sure. He conducted a crash course in Intimidation 101. Leo apparently felt that if he could scare a young umpire enough, he might get the benefit of any doubt in a few close calls.

The first postulate of the Leo Durocher Rule dictates that when a rookie is harassed by Durocher he *must* take off his face mask. This is a crucial theatrical device. If the umpire told Leo to pipe down with his face mask on, Durocher associated this with hiding behind the mask. An umpire had to maintain direct eye to eye contact with him.

The second postulate of the Rule demanded that a new umpire inform Durocher in no uncertain terms to shut up. You can't afford to be mealy-mouthed when Leo delivered a tirade of ugly diphthongs. The Durocher Rule worked best when both postulates were used in tandem. I became a master at this out of necessity. If Leo launched into a tirade when I was behind the plate, I took off my mask, went over to the dugout, waved my hand in his general direction, and shouted,"Aaaaaaaaaaah, shut up!!!!

Leo Durocher was one of the greatest baseball man to ever throw a conniption fit on the field. He thoroughly understood the mechanics of the game, and he was a shrewd and cunning strategist in the dugout, and he knew how to maximize his players' talents. But Leo's relationships with umpires was nearly on a par with the camaraderie shared between snakes and mongooses. It was all his side or nothing at all. I can still recall with clarity the lovely refrains of "Pryor, you blew it! You blew it!" as he charged onto the field.

Leo was a quick thinker on his feet and he could argue or lay claim to nearly any point even though it was supported with more stuffing than a Christmas turkey. During his tenure as manager of the Cubs, Leo conducted an interesting physiological seminar in the offices of National League President Warren Giles in Chicago. Cubs' pitcher Phil Regan had been accused of throwing spit balls and a hearing was set in Mr. Giles' office with Phil Regan, Durocher, and John Holland, General Manager of the Cubs.

Leo denied the fact that Reagan would even consider doctoring the ball. Perish the thought, Mr. Giles. He presented some physiological information he claimed to have received from the Mayo Clinic in Rochester, Minnesota. The latest scientific data Leo obtained announced that all men perspired under pressure. Hence, a biologically sound young man like Phil Regan pitching in front of untold millions of fans is apt to perspire on the mound. Regan can't help it, Durocher claimed. His only problem was that he was just human. If some sweat happened to get on Regan's ball, it was nothing more than a function of his metabolic process. After conducting his scientific seminar, Leo decided to drop the ball on Warren Giles' court.

"Look at yourself right now, Mr. Giles. You're perspiring on your forehead."

Warren Giles took a fast swipe process for head with his hand. Beads of sweat dangled from his fingers and dropped onto his desktop. Not an eye in the room missed a drop. The Phil Regan case was promptly closed.

Durocher was never short for words whenever it came to umpires. If he wasn't shouting a tirade from the dugout, he always had a creative wisecrack to deliver. Beneath that little chrome-domed head operated a fertile little factory of twisted wisdom.

I had first base duty one game when the umpires' equipment failed to arrive by game time. I put on a navy blue suit, a white shirt, and a black tie and strolled to the base to assume a position looking and feeling like a new priest. As I walked past Leo's dugout he noticed that I wasn't dressed in proper uniform. I knew the creative gears in his mind were working furiously and a crisp comment would soon be delivered.

"Hey, Paul," he called out while I was walking around the first base area.

I looked over to Durocher and awaited the result of his poignant observations. "What are you supposed to be today, a standup comedian?" he asked.

Despite the fact that Leo Durocher was an irascible, impossible curmudgeon who frequently use ugly, sesquipedalian words to umpires, I knew he still liked me. Many times when he was so mad that he could pull out whatever hair was left on his head, he'd charge up to me on the field and address me with a shout of "Jesus Christ!!!!!" after a few years of this, I began to think he was either terribly confused or just very sacrilegious. On the last occasion Leo addressed me as Jesus Christ, I stopped him before he could begin his tirade. "I'm not Jesus Christ!!!!!" I shouted at him. After I captured his attention with this remark, he piped down and I informed him in very plain, very quiet terms that I was not Jesus Christ, "but Peter, His right-hand man."

Leo's professional baseball career extended back to 1925 when he joined the New York Yankees' organization under the great Miller Huggins. Following a brief stint with the Cincinnati Redlegs and a tour with St. Louis when he dubbed the motley, but talented crew of Cardinals as "The Gas House Gang," he then joined Larry MacPhail's Dodgers and eventually became a player-manager, much to the surprise of third-base coach Babe Ruth who wanted a manager's job to cap an illustrious life in baseball. After a roller coaster ride in Ebbets Field, he signed on as skipper of the Giants in the Polo Grounds and managed the great rookie, Willie Mays. In the Sixties, Leo made a final, but exquisite encore with the Chicago Cubs. But for all of Durocher's bitter sweet baseball career that included a suspension from the sport for carousing with undesirables, all his great years of managing and his fine tactician's mind – he is the only manager I have ever known who destroyed his team's pennant chances because of a single play he ordered.

I remember the New York Mets when the only team in sorrier straits were the South Kosciusko Street Stains. There were good individual players that had come and gone with the Mets in those days, perhaps even the nucleus of a semi-reputable ball club, but nothing seemed to gel. On any given day, Casey Stengel was pacing the dugout scratching his already well-scratched head or relieving the attention of non-stop losing by taking a little snooze now and then.

In 1969, the "Amazing Mets" had finally left Hades for baseball's Heaven. Seaver, Grote, Koosman, Agee, and Staub provided the centerpiece for a great team. But until the last few weeks of that season, it looked as if Leo Durocher and the Chicago Cubs would win the National League's eastern division. With only two weeks left in the season, Durocher and company arrived in New York with a four or five game lead. During the last encounter of the teams at Wrigley, the Mets lost five or six games of that last series and looked bad.

But in the course of one of the games in Chicago, Tommy Agee hit a homerun. Leo had the memory of a bull elephant and did not take kindly to any Met popping one on Waveland Avenue near the end of a competitive season. Durocher was a practitioner of the Old Testament philosophy of "An eye for an eye, a tooth for a tooth." He didn't find any comfort in the corny notion of letting a sleeping dog lie and he was prepared to arbitrate matters on the field in New York.

When Tommy Agee came to bat during the two teams' last series together at Shea Stadium, Cubs' pitcher Bill Hands delivered a low-bridge throw and knocked him down. At that moment, something happened in the Mets' dugout. It was as though a canister of fireworks was ignited among them. The hometown players were braced on the first step of their dugout yelling, shouting, jumping up and down and crying foul. The sensation was electric and I could feel not only their anger and frustration across the field, but there seemed to be carried along these same airwaves a firm, resolve, a sudden, collective determination to win.

There may be a certain hit or an outstanding catch or play that, in hindsight, has been claimed to eclipse an important baseball event. Bobby Thomson's "Shot heard 'round the world" or Jackie Robinson's home plate steal are singular feats that have changed a team's complexion. Hands' low-bridge pitch to Agee sparked a nonchalant second-place squad of Mets into an excited team that came to quickly realize its potential – thanks to Leo Durocher.

Some veteran managers who have been around the ballpark a few tens of thousands of times know how to give the umpires the business without getting kicked out of the game. They drop a verbal bombshell without personally insulting an umpire to his face. This is a delicately learned study that requires a nimble mind and a lot of cultivation on the part of the manager. Former St. Louis manager Red Schoendinst was a master of this "lead balloon" technique.

I had second base duty for one game and called a Cardinal player out on a close play on the base. Red disagreed with the call he came out of the dugout to register his complaint.

"Pryor, what game are you watching?" Asked as he approached me.

I knew he was going to try to read me down country so I waited until he got closer to reply. "That was a real horse**** call you made, Pryor," Schoendinst told me.

Believe it or not, this is a strategic touché for a well-seasoned umpire. He didn't refer to *me* as the buy-product of a horse – just my call – and that makes all the difference in the world. Red knew how to give an umpire the bum's rush with all the dangling metaphors without ever ruffling the umpire directly.

The pre-game meeting between the home plate umpire and the two managers is actually much more than just an intimate formality. Line-up cards are presented and distributed between both managers and the umpire. A copy is forwarded to the game statistician. This obviously not only lets all parties involved know the place and position of both teams, but it helps prevent any incident of a player batting out of order.

Most of the talk at the meeting is devoted to the stadium's ground rules. Opposing managers will usually rattle them off the same way they are presented on the back of the home team's scorecard.

The meeting before the first game of a series is usually the longest. The ground rules are thoroughly covered for the benefit of the opposing manager. During the course of a season's chase, many of the subtle rules between ballparks can become blurry. If an opposing manager or coach forgets about some ground rule, a player may be stopped at second because the visiting team mistakenly thinks he is only entitled to a double on a certain hit instead of continuing his route around the base paths. The opposing manager's interest and attention span usually wanes geometrically at the meeting before the second, third, or fourth game of the series.

Some managers reluctantly trudge to the meeting as if they'd been summoned to address a convention of lepers. Other detail-oriented managers like Gene Mauch cling onto every word as if it were gospel and then take notes. Casey Stengel had more twists and turns in his ground rule monologue that could be imagined. I never knew if he was legitimately crisscrossed on the rules of the old Polo Grounds or whether he was purposefully confusing the umpires and opposing managers just for laughs, but Stengel's ground rules were totally different from the park's rules. For the first game of a Mets series he'd say that a "second" step in one part of the stadium was a homerun. The following day he claimed that a second step for the first sort of hit in the same part of the Polo Grounds was a double. Then he'd swear on his authenticity. I think Casey would scout his roster to determine what batter was hot at that time, cross-match it with his field of hitting preference, and then fabricate a special stadium ground rule.

Sometimes he would just resort to playing doubletalk and use every obscure term in the lexicon of baseball in the process. One day in the Pole Grounds, Casey gave an especially creative rendition of ground rules. He was speaking enthusiastically about how a ball hit before the form, but after the turn, entitled the hitter to one base before the triform. He repeated his tale for the benefit of the opposing manager and me without skipping a beat. After listening to this a second time with even less clarity than the first, I decided to take matters into my own hands. I knew that if I asked Casey for a reasonable translation, the game wouldn't start until nighttime or maybe not even until the swallows returned to Central Park. After I'd heard enough, I told Casey, "in other words, we're just going to play ball and will play by *my* rules today." The opposing manager was in complete agreement with my decision and the game perilously began.

After the official business of exchanging line-up cards and reviewing the ground rules is completed, sometimes the tripartite at home plate will engage in a little humor. During one game in Cincinnati between the Reds and the Mets, every pigeon east of the Mississippi decided to roost for the day in Riverfront Stadium. While squadron after squadron performed reconnaissance flights over the field, Mets' manager Gil Hodges and Reds captain Pete Rose and I went all through the process of exchanging line-cards and reviewing the ground rules. The sheer number of pigeons around Riverfront Stadium made me think that at least one of these urban-based flying rats was destined to intimately meet a pop fly. At the conclusion of the pre-game meeting, I looked up at the small dark clouds of pigeons and created a special ground rule for the occasion. My concern with the ominous skies caused Rose and Hodges to up look up into the Cincinnati skies. I addressed Rose because he was the representative of the home team. "Pete, if a hit is made and it happens to bang a male pigeon in the air, a man is entitled to two bases and two bases only.

Pete perused the heavens and then looked at me seriously. "Paul, what happens if someone hits a female?

"Well, then it's all you can get." He looked at me as if he expected a squad of ornithologists from the University of Cincinnati to come parading into the stadium at any moment.

Between both leagues, there seems to be a reasonable balance with managers who have particular specialties. No league is particularly predominated or populated with strategists, rules experts, or clowns. In all my years in the National League, I've discovered that not only are any two managers in the least alike in temperament, but each has his own very special acumen of the game.

Foremost amongst a host of all sorts of qualities both good and bad, Leo Durocher was a master strategist. He knew how to tap a player's talents and exact the maximum performance from virtually every man on his roster. Each player in the field was like a strategic move on a master chessboard that Leo had to react to. Despite the fact that he was an irascible manager who'd perform any antic to win and a ne'er-do-well off the field, Leo was a coy tactician and a formidable opponent, no matter what team he faced.

Gene Mauch was the epitome of managers who are "rules men." He knew baseball's legislation inside and out, backwards and forwards. In fact, no National League manager would like to confront Gene in a Rule Book quiz. He knew even the most obscure, arcane rule of the game and used it if he could benefit his team. Besides the rules of the road, Gene understood the human side of the game and was a tireless worker in the dugout. If God really did give whiskey to the Irish to keep them from taking over the world, then He bestowed Gene Mauch with an over-abundance of talent so he'd over-manage the Phillies. Gene would over-orchestrate his Phillies teams even if they were knocking on the pennant door.

Walter Alston was a master at advancing his players around the bases. During his successful career as a manager, the Dodgers were perhaps the best hit and run team in the National League. Once he was able to get some of his speedsters on the bases, his next task was to manipulate runners to home plate. Although there were better brute-strength teams in the league, Alston utilized every chip shot, Texas leaguer, base on balls, and outfield fly to eke out victories.

Bill Virdon, the former great Pirates outfielder, was also a great manager. Bill ran the Expos, Astros, Pirates, in Yankees on the field. He knew how to extract the most from his players and like Gene Mauch, he was a rules expert. Unfortunately, Bill was hired by the four franchises just when they seemed to perform a talent somersault. Sometimes he had mediocre starters and a good bullpen. On other occasions, his teams were stacked with sluggers and a poor complement of pitchers. Offenses were sometimes good while defenses were poor. The front offices seem to rapidly grow impatient and Bill was never retained long enough to prove his worth.

Joe Amalfatano was another strategist who was given a stopwatch treatment by the Cubs' organization. Instead of naturally turning the Cubbies into National League east winners in time, he was plucked from the dugout prematurely. Most of the positive changes he instituted en route to building a solid club were unraveled by his successor and altered according to his own philosophy.

John McNamara is another example of a great manager who never seemed to get the kind of horses he needed for a successful run. He capitalized on his players' special abilities and each member of a McNamara team knew that hustling was a prerequisite to any action on the field. Against the more talented team, Mac usually fought back by out-hustling his opponents and creating mistake situations to pounce on.

Strategic foresight is a major asset that distinguishes a good manager from former players and baseballphiles who think they could run a team. Winning managers look at each play with the tactical eye and assess the likely consequences of events in the near future. They know the particular gifts of each man on the team as well as a working knowledge of the opposition, and construct a play according to the given set of information on the field at any given moment in time. Each offensive and defensive move changes the disposition of strategy. Hence, a good manager must be adept in devising a movable strategy capable of successfully countering the dodges and shifts of his opponent one batter or one pitch in advance. Former Hall of Fame players and superstars may thoroughly know the mechanics of baseball, but unless they can strategically orchestrate a game, they're only a team's big-name cheerleader.

A lot of managers are unwilling to stand by a mediocre player. A good manager tries to determine if a merely adequate player has untapped potential or even whether a change of attitude can accent his performance. At best, Tim Foley was only an average player with the Expos and the Mets. He was a chronic complainer on the field who liked to blame a poor performance on an umpire's call. He believed that if the umpire only made honest calls, he'd have a reasonable shot at becoming a team leader. When Foley joined the Pirates' organization, it looked as if his move to Pittsburgh would be a short-lived and final end to a modest career. But Pirates' manager Chuck Tanner felt that if Foley could just play without the imagined retinue of excuses, he could become a star. Thanks to Tanner and Dave Parker's suggestions, Tim learn to shut up on the field and play the game. Let the umpires umpire and you just play were Parker's words of wisdom. That season, Foley came into his own and played an instrumental role in the Pirates' championship.

There is usually a very predictable sequence of dramatic scenes that takes place from the time an irate manager leaves the dugout until the time he is banished from the field. Scene One is nominally the Confrontation stage of the drama. This is when the concerned manager runs on the field. A call has just been made that he disagrees with. At this point, the manager is psychologically prepared to engage the umpire in a debate in hopes of somehow reversing the call. Hope springs eternal – little does he know that the chances of a reversal are infinitesimal but he'll argue his point valiantly.

The next scenario is usually the Argument. This is when frustration and desperation override his hopes of reasoning with the umpire. His point was acknowledged, but flatly rejected. Now anger runneth over as he is about to lose his head gasket. He's mad as hell and there's nothing he can do about it! Now the fun part begins.

The Retaliation stage is the most dangerous part of tête-à-tête. The manager feels that he has been capriciously dealt a hand of outrageous justice and he's about to do something about it. At this juncture, it's usually difficult for an umpire to determine exactly what path of retaliation a manager will take. Some guys will dance around in momentary hysteria and perform one of the antics that automatically buys a front seat on the Hindenburg. Throwing bats, bumping the umpire, kicking dirt on the umpire or the plate, stealing second base and misappropriating it in his dugout – he knows all the overt tricks that bounce him from the park, but he's so damn mad at this point he could care less. Screamers will search their minds for anything they may know about an umpire and use sinful similes about his parentage, ancestry, religion, or any anti-cultural social habits. When the umpire has heard enough, he points a thumb to the manager's dugout.

The Invective stage or the "By the way, one other thing…" scene occurs only with some managers. Many will just mumble and parade to the showers. Others know they've just been bought an expensive ride out of the park, but they're still not psychologically prepared to acquiesce to the umpire's final judgment. On the way off the field, some managers will turn around and give a final verbal rebuke to the umpire. "By the way, I never really did like you, so don't ever, ever speak to me again!" is the tenor of their departing words of wisdom. The Invective scenario is usually the manager's time to inform the umpire how he really feels about him. The call on the field seems of no relevance and the umpire becomes the sole target of his wrath. Fans can follow the stages of the CARI sequence just by observing the body language of the umpire and manager. Real students of the sport may elect to take a lip reading course for the full dramatic impact.

Once I had the first base assignment for the Opening game at Riverfront Stadium. The Reds are the oldest, consecutively operating franchise major league baseball. Traditionally, the first ball of the first game of the season is tossed in Cincinnati. During spring training several weeks earlier, I invited Sparky Anderson to be the keynote speaker for a sports benefit at my new parish in St. Petersburg, Florida. Sparky was already the successful manager of the colossal Big Red Machine and I was a seasoned National League umpire. We had seen enough of one another through the years that we eventually became friends on and off the field.

During the first inning, the pitcher performed a shuffle step away from the mound rubber and I called a balk. Evidently, Sparky was watching a completely different thing from the dugout and he charged onto the field to give me his rendition. "Pryor, don't you know what a balk is???!!! Don't you know what a balk is???!!! he screamed time and again. The Confrontation phase of the CARI principle was well underway.

He then went through a detailed rendition of Fred Astaire choreography and illustrated his point with a few cute dance numbers of his own. I listened to his argument and told him that from my vantage point besides first, the pitcher had balked. Period. I wasn't going to change my call no matter what he saw.

The Retaliation scene began with a whirlwind of choice expletive deleted. He no longer was thinking about the balk, but how I was a no good ugly mixed metaphor. After I'd heard enough, I gave him the thumb in front of the Opening Day crowd toward the preferred personnel portal.

If Sparky was furious just a moment earlier, his head gasket took leave of his neck now. As he marched out of the park, I knew he was turning over thoughts of me. Finally the Invective stage took place as he performed an about-face with a laser-powered index finger directed at me. "And another thing," he screamed, "Don't you ever, ever, ask me to come to one of your benefits again – not when it's going to cost me money to get thrown out of the game!!!"

There will always be a special place in my chest protector for those managers who vehemently disagreed with one of my calls, but decided to endure their dark night of the soul in the dugout rather than fight the field. The dugout floors are littered with their pulled hair. Instead of publicly demonstrating their frustration, they rant and rave at umpires from the protected area of the dugout. I could never determine exactly why they'd only complain from the dugouts instead of charging onto the field like the Durocher's and Weaver's of the baseball world. Perhaps they were naturally shy and preferred yanking their hair in the privacy of their own front porch.

Herman Franks, the former Cubs and Giants manager took a very ecclesiastical approach to umpires. If I made a call he objected to on the field, Herman would stalk the dugout with his arms raised in a 45° angle like some medieval pope in benediction and complained bitterly. When I finally reached my tolerance threshold, I turned to his dugout and yelled out, "Hey, Herman, shut up!!" His next reaction was so predictable that I've staged time and again in my mind. He'd raise both arms in prayer, fingertips vaulted together, to indicate his innocence. Frequently he looked like the Pontiff in St. Peter's Square as he walked with this reverent pose back and forth in the dugout.

The manager's role in the ball club's hierarchy has changed dramatically over the years. Thirty or forty years ago, before revolving doors were installed in front of their offices, managers were very much a part of the team's autocracy. In effect, they were management's field stewards for the front offices. While Leo Durocher still ran the Dodgers just after World War II, he was paid $50,000 to manage the Brooklyn Bums when many of his players were only receiving ten, twelve, or thirteen thousand dollars a year. Even the teams' stars looked up to the managers in those days as highly paid representatives of the owners. Players were treated like blue-collar labor men with lunch pails. If they didn't like the conditions or the salary, they could join pop behind the plow back home. Home

CHAPTER SEVEN

PITCHERS

"Paul loved to see people from Woonsocket. He'd put them up overnight and bring them to the clubhouse to meet all the players. Paul was outgoing, friendly, gregarious just a big, happy-go-lucky Guy. " -Long-time friend Dick Dwyer

Players divide home plate umpires into two prime categories. Besides the classifications of bad and worse, "there are umpires who are considered "pitchers'" umpires and those looked up as "hitters'" umpires.

Supposedly a pitchers' umpire gives the benefit of the doubt to the pitcher on a throw that is a borderline call between a strike and a ball. Instead of second guessing, this particular breed of umpire may be inclined to call a fence-sitting pitch a strike.

The hitters' umpire usually feels sorry for the guy in the batters' box. I could never understand this simply because the batter was holding a large hunk of sculpted wood in his hands. He could be lethal with it if he wanted to. But the hitters' umpire is more inclined to favor the batter in a half-ball, half-strike situation. This breed of umpire obviously believes the pitcher has an inherent advantage. He's the character on an unusual, raised pile of dirt, throwing a very hard ball inches away from the soft bones and head of a hitter. Both categories of umpire feel their call preferences are an effort to neutralize the inherent advantages of either the batter or the pitcher.

I have never known an umpire to flaunt either classification. Most will not even admit that there are such creatures as hitters' more pitchers' umpires. It's more a subtle inclination on their part to slightly favor one position or the other in a borderline situation.

I was inclined to favor the pitcher and toss-up situations. Home plate is only seventeen inches wide and the circumference of the baseball is just nine inches. The pitcher has a grand total of twenty-six inches to work with. This is no simple task considering he is throwing from 60' 6" away. In the back of my mind, of course are a number of memories I had as a professional pitcher. In hindsight, it seemed awfully hard to throw a lot of strikes. Awfully hard. And it gets lonely on the mound. The strike zone can seem to get smaller and smaller each inning until it appears to be the size of a shoebox and a manager decides to send you to the showers long before you're even dirty. This feeling does little to help a pitcher's psyche. The sensation a pitcher gets when he's been shelled on the mound in an important game with the team relying on a top performance is akin to being slapped across the face by your fiancé when your mother is watching.

One telltale method of determining the difference between these two schools of umpires is the way they call pitches that cross the black perimeter of the plate. Surrounding Abner Doubleday's strange pentagon is a black border. If a throw crossed this black edge of the plate, I usually gave the strike to the pitcher. A batters' umpire would probably side with the hitter.

A ballgame will tend to move at a quicker pace when an umpire more inclined to the pitchers' zone works the plate. Many four-hour extravaganzas are the handiwork of batter-favored umpires. The pitchers throw more strikes, the batters have more opportunities to wait for "their" pitches, on-deck hitters report to the team trainers with age-induced arthritis.

People are curious why umpires examine so many baseballs during the course of the game. I've been asked why I had to scrutinize baseballs as if they might contain gold fillings between the stitches. Actually, what I looked for were scuffs, scratches, dirt bruises, or any kind of obtuse substance an imaginative pitcher could use to make the ball perform unusual aerial acrobatics. Basically, baseballs are checked by umpires to ensure their playing integrity because any re-facing of a ball can potentially change its flight pattern.

The airborne route of any spheroid object can be changed by attaching a foreign object or substance to it. In fact, even the stitches on a baseball can make it travel quite differently from a ball of the same weight and diameter with a totally smooth surface. The application of any additional weight changes the rotation, trajectory, direction, even the speed of the ball, so that an incoming pitch flying on one vector suddenly seems to get educated about the bat and performs strange avoidance moves.

Over the years, creative pitchers have also discovered other means of doctoring a ball without adding anything to it. There is another equally coy school of mound magicians I call the "detractors" who take something off the balls' surfaces. The repeated puncturing of the leather skin with a thumbtack will change the modus operandi of the pitch. Slicing a number of stitches to accent a curveball is another common technique. Any sufficiently sharp object tucked in the hinterlands of the pitcher's glove or the sly swipe made by the catcher against his sharpened kneepads can fix a ball.

Scuffed baseballs of reasonable throwing value are normally removed from the game and stockpiled for the home team's batting practices. Cut or badly bruised balls are sent to the trash heaps of baseball history along with the vendors' hot dog rinds in cardboard beer cups. Ultimately, any scuffed ball that remains in play will serve as an advantage to the pitcher. Umpires will normally check balls hit to any part of the stadium. A foul that hits the backstop can easily be cut or the double that meets the brick wall at Wrigley Field will probably not be suited for further use.

Any experienced umpire in either league would probably determine which stadium the ball was played in if he had a dirt smudge from the home plate area to examine. Baseball dirt is by no means the common, garden-variety material beneath most shoes. Each stadium has its own peculiar consistency and color dirt. One park will have gray, sandy soil, another's topsoil may be clay-like and sable-colored. Probably the dirt in the Dodger Stadium is the easiest to recognize and the most unusual. Any pitch that bounced off the soil or around home plate in Los Angeles will wear a nice, bright, red clay streak.

I now realize that when I was cut from the Georgia State League, I should have become a diver in Chesapeake Bay instead of an umpire. Only the occasional barracuda would abuse me and I'd make a lot of money playing Jacques Cousteau for the major leagues.

A special gray mud from the Chesapeake Bay is used by major league umpires to prepare baseballs. Instead of umpires applying the strange stadium topsoil's of varying consistency, the gray mud standardizes the prep treatment. The dirt also has the unique texture of removing the protective lacquer-like finish from the ball, without affecting its surface quality.

But the most amazing feature of this mud is not its unique consistency, but its price. Per ounce, it is somewhere between gold and platinum on the Mineral Exchange. A small bucket of it costs in excess of $35!! For 20 years I was treated like dirt when I could have been dredging it all along!!

The unusual rotation of the ball is the umpire's best indication of doctoring. Because the ball is not pushed or catapulted, every ball that leaves the pitchers' hands has a rotation pattern to it. Any additive or terror becomes effective only as the ball goes its rotation process. The "normal" rotation scheme is distorted depending on any additive or slice. A cut ball will usually effect the lateral motion of the ball. A substantial slice will ultimately cause a ball to move either to the left or right of the batter like a curveball. Hence, a curveball pitcher is more apt to cut the ball in some way to put a real bend to his throw.

The application of a heavy substance like toothpaste, Vaseline, or mud will make the ball drop as it approaches the plate. A fastball pitcher may opt for this method if he finds his throws beginning to rise into the sluggers' zones. A sinkerball man who finds himself losing the knack to bow before the plate might dab his baseball with a little magic mischief to keep it zinging towards the catcher's toes.

A good mound doctor works hard at his furtive expertise. It takes a lot of practice to know how much of a certain substance will alter the conduct of a pitch. Not only does he have to select the substance in proper quantities, but he has to know how to throw his concoction. Sometimes the delivery movement may be different and the fingers may be spaced tighter or further apart to perform his job. Once the prescription is determined, the next task for the pitcher is to learn how to apply the substance without being detected. He might be ingenious when it comes to determining the additive, but he also must be downright sneaky to execute his plans in front of the opposing team, umpires, and an untold number of fans.

The detractors have to go through similar research and development sessions. Not any size will perform the job. Just the right length depth and position of the cut is important. A scar too close to the stitches will not be as effective as one through an "open" part of the ball.

Many major league pitchers are devout students of a baseball's peculiar nuances. Some hurlers who would never consider throwing a doctored pitch will look at each new ball and determine if for any unusual eccentricities. Both leagues use baseballs that are hand sewn in Haiti. Because the human element is directly involved in the creation of each baseball, sometimes the stitching is not even. Some clean pitchers will throw back unevenly stitched ball to the umpire. Others will utilize the uneven sewing to accent the curve ball they intended on throwing.

I think that some of the most persnickety and superstitious ballplayers somehow find their way to pitching staffs. Hurlers have all sorts of bizarre idiosyncrasies that they cannot even explain. I've thrown new balls to pitchers and had them immediately rejected. I've inspected new baseballs and toss them out of play for the same reaction. Then I returned the same ball that was just rejected by the pitcher and it was taken with a great thanks.

Warren Spahn was the most selective pitcher I've ever umpired. He insisted that the trademark had to be rubbed off each ball before he would consider throwing it. Filing down the National League stamp and president's signature had never been mentioned in my job description. I think when most of the league umpires discovered they had home plate duty with Spahn on the mound, they prayed for rain instead of Johnny Sain.

Chris Short of the Phillies was another finicky pitcher who could drive a strong umpire to drink. He seemed to have a rigid set of criteria for each ball pasted to him, but no one could determine exactly what it was. Short would reject ball after ball until I was tempted to grab the bat from the hitter and perform an umpiring first the pitcher's mound. Then I got smart and threw back some of the same old balls he had just brandished – and accepted them graciously.

Pete Rose has a jeweler's eye for the phony pitches. If a sinker suspiciously drops off the table or a curve bends beyond normal expectations, Pete usually isn't shy about asking the home plate umpire to examine the ball. Unfortunately, the catcher gladly obliges – but only after he's twisted the ball a few times in his mitt.

Whenever Phil Regan of the Cubs was pitching against the Reds, Pete usually paid particular attention to each throw.

Regan's reputation as a spitter preceded him and Pete studied each delivery like a pitching scout.

During one game, Regan through a sinker that looked as if it was attached to a bowling ball. Pete stepped out of the batter's box and stared at me for a long moment. "It dropped off the table," he said calmly. "He's throwing a spitter."

I examined the ball after the catcher had the opportunity to twist any incriminating evidence into his glove. I couldn't find anything wrong with the ball.

"Pete, if he's throwing a spitter and I eject him from the game, will you be a witness at the hearing?" I asked.

"What hearing?" Rose piped back sharply.

"Well, nowadays if you accuse a picture of doctoring the ball, he's entitled to a hearing at the League offices. Will you be a witness at the hearing?"

"Oh, no, no, no, no," he fired back in his special staccato voice as he stepped back into the batterers' box. Pete was never much for the bureaucratic aspects of the game.

A cornucopia of materials have been discovered on phony balls. Band-Aids, toothpaste, Vaseline, thumbtacks, slices across the league stamp – the list is virtually endless. The real coy operators probably have some formidable devices, but their technics remain secret. They're so good that they've never been caught! These are the pitchers that could earn extra money and help their country during the off-season by working for the CIA.

Many pitchers have been accused of doctoring their baseballs, fewer have been nabbed, and only a handful have actually come out of their closets on the mound to deliver an admission of guilt. Gaylord Parry and Don Sutton are two of the more renowned pitcher-physicians. I knew Sutton was tampering with his baseballs, but I never caught him red-handed. After one game Don pitched for the Cincinnati Reds, I rummaged through the fouled balls to determine the discards and batting practice counts. There were about 30 balls that all had a slice through the National League stamp and president's signature. I thought that perhaps with the slit on the ball, Don was able to throw a certain pitch that batterers normally fouled to accumulate a strike count. I was never able to find a sliced ball in either his glove or his catcher's.

Rick Honeycutt of the Seattle Mariners was thrown out of the game and fined for throwing bogus balls in 1980. Rick was a practitioner of the detractor school of mound medicine. Evidently, he had a thumbtack hidden in his glove and between pitches managed to puncture the skin enough to make it perform acrobatics on its way to the plate.

There are more purported ways Whitey Ford doctored the ball than there are fleas on a junkyard dog. If only 10% were true then Whitey was undoubtedly the most notorious covert doctor to ever stand atop a mound. It is also indicative of the fact that he is the slyest operator in baseball history because he was never caught in the act.

One report claimed that Whitey's pitches involved a conspiratorial effort by the whole Yankee team. Supposedly, one of Yogi Berra's kneepads was sharpened so that a quick brush with the ball created a slice. A ball caught in the outfield was rubbed against a small sharpened straight edge hidden in the gloves and nonchalantly returned to Whitey on the mound.

My umpire source told me that Ford, in fact, was a mud pack man. According to this account, he took moist mound dirt and packed it between the stitches, thus weighing down the ball and enabling it to perform the sort of tricks he wanted it to. But unless Whitey ever decides to come clean with his covert techniques, his mysteries will continue to be clouded by wild speculation.

I tip my hat to Gaylord Perry, Don Sutton, Bill Singer, Phil Regan, Lou Burdette, and Don Cardwell – and all the rest of the masters of the phony ball both apprehended and undetected for your brilliant Dog Henning imitations. I only wish I had been good enough to catch you red-handed!!!

In 1968, the National League decided to put the whammy on the medical corpsman of the various pitching staffs. Umpires are always on guard against this sort of activity, but during this particular year, the National League put special emphasis on examining suspect pitchers for foreign materials. But like most half-hearted directives from the league offices, and umpire's attempts at enforcement are only wrought with frustration. Despite the fact that umpires are employees of the league and players and managers work for teams, rarely will the league president side with the umpire with a discrepancy on the field. Unless a player's actions are so overt that people in the stands and before their television sets are witness to the abuse dealt an umpire, the league hierarchies will usually stand by the player. Major league baseball pays tremendous lip service to enforcing the law on the field, but when an umpire tries to effectively police a game, his call for disciplinary action is largely ignored by the Leagues.

Augie Donatelli was behind the plate for a game that year between the Dodgers and the Braves when he noticed something very suspicious about Don Drysdale's pitches. The ball was performing more aerial acrobatics in route to the plate then the Flying Burrito Brothers on stage.

Augie stopped the game and went to the mound to inspect Drysdale. "Let me see your hat," he demanded. Drysdale stood up as straight as he could on the rubber and refused to let him inspect his cap. Augie jumped up a few times as if he was trying to tap a rimmer into a basketball hoop.

Augie Donatelli is a stately 5'10" and socks and shoes. Drysdale is nothing less than a towering 6' 6". Somehow the odds didn't especially favor Augie's side of the argument.

Angered by his unsuccessful rebounding attempts, Augie delivered the ultimatum. Either Drysdale relinquish his lid for inspection or be injected from the game. Period. Don surrendered the suspicious chapeau and Augie took a good hard look for grease, tar, pitch, Vaseline, crazy glue, or any of the other sundry batch of creative ingredients the M.A.S.H. units sometimes use. In the end, Augie couldn't find anything incriminating.

The sports section of the next day's paper carried a cute little cartoon depicting Augie bouncing high in attempts to reach Drysdale's cap. "Umpire missed his mark," read the caption.

Augie was infuriated about the incident, but it wasn't the cartoon that set him off. The mere fact that he was performing his job on the field and receiving no cooperation for his efforts from the high brass of baseball was more than a little disheartening.

Without a doubt, pitchers are the most scrutinized players in the game. Outside of the third-base umpire, the three other partners on the diamond maintain a beat on the pitcher's actions. While the home plate umpire calls balls and strikes, the men assigned first and second base duty observe the pitcher for balks if runners are on base.

The balk call is a small modification in the game that compensates for the pitchers' inherent advantage with runners. If there was no balk, base running without a corresponding hit would be virtually impossible. A pitcher could theoretically pivot himself midway through his wind up and toss the ball to the runner's holding base.

The great majority of balks are either the result of an experienced pitcher's temporary loss of concentration or an inexperienced pitcher's overzealous attempt to instantly make the runner on base a memory. But a veteran pitcher usually has a carefully trained footwork pattern on the mound. His leg movements and push off the rubber are designed to accommodate the pitch. It is as significant to the final outcome of the throw as the way the ball is held and released. A pitch delivered without the proper leg balance and thrust will be an unsuccessful pitch. The top half of the body must work in tandem with the stability and power offered by the lower half of the body.

A seasoned umpire can usually follow the choreography of the veteran pitcher relatively easily. In fact, the great base runners like Lou Brock, Maury Wills, and Ricky Henderson follow the leg movements of a pitch the same way as first base umpires. Their footwork becomes something of a signature that is recognized in time. Runners will look for any suspicious, momentary hesitations in their pattern that might be a clue to a toss to the bag.

Other pitchers naturally have a garbled leg pattern. This is nothing more or less than their style. Legs seem to twitch and dance without reason and often it is difficult to determine if the pitcher is trying to make a sly move to first or whether he is just dancing his way to the plate.

Lou Burdette had more gyrations on the mound than the Pope on Christmas. He had a variety of deliveries that included a choreographed dance of leg twitching, arm jerking, and neck movements. With a man on first base, an umpire had to keep a close watch on Burdette's prancing feet in relation to the rubber.

Once in Pittsburgh, Lou was on the mound with runners on first and second base. He began his Neanderthal ritual and threw the ball to first. I thought his foot was still on the rubber and called a balk.

The game came to a halt while the runners on first and second advance to their next bases. Lou Burdette and Manager Birdie Tebbetts were "convinced" his foot was off the rubber and they screamed bloody murder. Tebbetts' argument was plain and simple. With all his dance movements, how in the hell could an umpire possibly determine if Burdette's foot was on the rubber? Was I a dance contest judge, or an umpire?

Frank Secory was my second base partner and as I glanced over in his direction, he gave me a covert signal that indicated Burdette's foot was off the rubber when he threw to first. From his position, he actually had a better view of Lou's dance number than me. I came to the decision that the runners and batterers should return to their respective paces and a balk would not be given to Burdette. I would have disagreed with my fellow umpires' decision to revoke the call if Lou Burdette had not been on the mound. He was one of those rare pitchers who demand either telescopic vision or super-umpire qualities to legitimately determine if he committed a balk.

My decision to countermand the balk and return the runners immediately ruined Pirates' manager Danny Murtaugh's whole day. Scene III, Stage Pittsburgh, just began as Murtaugh charged onto the field and read me the Riot Act. I listened through a hazy spray of chewing tobacco to a laundry list of tirades.

"Paul, you can't change your mind! I would have disagreed with my fellow umpires You just can't change your mind!! He kept yelling.

One minute the Pirates' fans thought I was the greatest thing since gingersnaps because of my balk call, while the next minute I was the walking plague.

Convincing Danny Murtaugh that I did, in fact, absolutely, positively, change my mind made me feel like Ripley telling yet another unbelievable story. No sooner did Danny returned to the Pirates' dugout then I heard a strange course of jungle noises from the stands call out, "balk, balk, balk, balk!! For the next few series I umpired in Pittsburgh, I became accustomed to the serenade of, "There's Paul Pryor. It's all balk, balk, balk, balk, balk!!!"

Al Hrabosky went through more gyrations, gesticulations, and more periods of physical perturbation than any other major league pitcher who ever pushed off a mound. "The Mad Hungarian" had a unique way of stimulating his pitching psyche between pitches and batterers.

Al was always considered something of a "cult of one" when he broke into the majors. I think he heard some of the Eternal Voices most of us have never paid too much attention to. Between pitches Al went through a self-psych ceremony where he would walk off the mound toward second base, study the turf between his feet, and then repeatedly smack the ball into his glove. Once he conversed with The Spirits, Al would return to the mound, look at the threesome of batter, catcher, and umpire through the eyes of Rasputin and finally, finally, throw the ball.

There is an arcane little role in baseball that most fans, even devoted fans are usually not aware of. A pitcher is required to throw a pitch within twenty seconds after receiving it back from the catcher when there are no men on base. The penalty for throwing beyond the allotted time is a ball added to the batter's count. Twenty seconds doesn't seem like very much time, but with no men on base, it still gives a pitcher a lot of time to perform his private warm-up and prep session.

I was umpiring second base in St. Louis when Hrabosky left the mound for a ball pounding ceremony. I watched him wheeze and tweeze for a while until I glanced at my stopwatch and realize he had only a few more seconds to deliver his pitch.

"You got about three more seconds to throw the ball!!," I called out from my vantage point beside second base.

Hrabosky quickly packed the ball into his glove, ran to the mound, and hastily delivered a premature pitch that ended up in the dirt.

Immediately afterward, he accused me of destroying his concentration. I had to deliver an impromptu rulebook lesson before he calmed down enough to return to the mound. I just followed the rules. C'est la guerre, mon frere.

Pitchers get all sorts of extraneous help from their catchers. If a spitter's on the mound, his catcher is not only a co-conspirator, but he must know how to rid the ball of its doctoring substance if the umpire demands an examination. Usually a catcher will twist the ball generously in his mitt a few times before turning the suspect ball over to the home plate umpire. If the dynamic duo is broken apart because of a free-agency move or a trade, their next encounter as opponents can be amusing. I've been behind the plate when catchers have stepped out of the batter's box and informed me when a pitcher is doctoring the ball. "How do you know for sure?" I've asked. "Because, I can tell by the throw. It's moving the same way as when I caught for him – and believe me, he was doctoring it then!!"

Sparky Anderson and Johnny Bench of the Cincinnati Reds had a unique routine that drove umpires to the brink of insanity. Bench played the straight man behind the plate as he caught while Sparky did the vocals from the dugout in a unique kind of Frick and Frack routine.

Johnny would grab a pitch just outside the strike zone and quickly move his glove within the strike zone. This was a slick, split-second maneuver known in the trade as "sucking-in the ball." Bench held the ball that extra moment in his glove to show fans, coaches, and managers how the umpire was incorrectly calling bonafide strikes.

Meanwhile, back in the dugout, Sparky is watching the "strikes" zoom down the alley and begins riding the umpire. "Where's the pitch? Hah? Where's the pitch? Where's the pitch, ump?" It's occasions like this that prompt the umpire to let the catcher know he's sucking-in the ball. But if the routine is putting enough pressure on the official behind the plate, he'll usually continue the practice until a confrontation with the manager ensues.

Home plate umpires can usually tell when a hurler is losing his edge even before the pitching coach in the dugout. Fastball pitchers tend to deliver the balls higher into the batter's prime zones. Curves and sliders either curve and slide at the wrong time or not at all. Knuckleball pilots lose their throttle and pump their pitches all over the home plate area. Control experts lose their innate guidance mechanism and begin aiming the ball and wondering if the club house attendant have a clean towel and a fresh bar of soap by their locker.

Pitchers get edgy and defensive when they realize their throws are not working according to plans. They frequently throw their hands up in frustration or sarcastically insist that the ump keep a closer watch on their pitches because the close call was diagnosed a ball. Pitchers become superstitious during this precarious time. Most know that they've temporarily lost their edge and hope that with a little poise, concentration, and luck they'll recoup the strike zone. Other sulk in quiet desperation as they began to see flashes of home runs launched in their mind's eye.

Don Elston of the Chicago Cubs used to perform a uniquely choreographed hand-arm routine when he was in trouble on the mound. Everyone on my crew knew him as "George Washington" because he loved to survey the ball. When Elston began to lose his stuff on the mound, he tried to correct my judgment by indicating where the ball actually was through his arm movements. If I called a ball because his throw was too high, he pointed down to the ground to indicate it was slower than I thought. I'd respond by giving him the high sign to confirm my call. After each pitch he'd redirect the call with his hands and I respond with my own arm signals. Fans had absolutely no idea what was going on between the two of us on the field. Unless they knew exactly what Elston was trying to indicate it looked as though he was making obscene gestures to the three men huddled around the plate. Perhaps I shouldn't have encouraged him with my return gestures, but it was usually so funny that I couldn't help but enjoy this Tweedledum-Tweedledee routine. These point, counter-pointing bouts usually went on until Don was asked by the Cubs manager to take an early shower.

Just about every pitcher in the majors has some version of a fastball and curve. They may not always be that fast or break that much, but both pitches are common in the big league arsenals. There is also a unique sociological strata hitters attribute to the different kinds of pitchers. Good fastball pitchers and curveball artists are the elite of the pitching staffs. These are the guys with "the right stuff." By their ability to throw very fast and confuse a batter's timing or make a ball bend hard to one side or another, they are the premier pilots of the mound. Nothing can be as exhilarating for a home plate umpire than calling balls and strikes when both of these specialists are in top form. On the bottom rungs of this pitching hierarchy are the sinkerball men and even below that, the lowly knuckleballers.

Sinkerball pitchers have the misfortune of being accused of doctoring the ball even when they're not. A bona fide sinker expert can make the ball "drop off the table" when he is most effective. Not only will the ball sink as it approaches the plate, but it will make something of a dramatic nose dive just before it reaches the perimeter of the bat's radius. An effective sinker requires a tremendous amount of skill and it can be as adept at deceiving hitters as virtually any other pitch that exists. But the sinker has little flair and is essentially a "boring" pitch from the perceptive of the hitter.

Koufax, Seaver, Ryan, Gibson, and Marichel were among some of the fastest pitchers I umpired in the National League. It was always interesting to have home plate duty when Juan Marichel pitched because he had about three or four different fastball speeds. He'd throw two of his swiftest pitches and then downshift a gear to a fastball that completely ridiculed the batter's timing.

A few fastball pitchers had the ability to make a ball "sail." This is the sudden upward lift of a ball just before it approaches the plate area. An eager batter would see a delectable fastball rocket down the groove of the strike zone and swing for the Northwest Territories. About forty-five degrees through his swing, the ball seemed to catch a thermal uplift and carry it above the latitude of the bat. Bob Gibson was a craftsman of the sailer. I'd seen him throw hundreds of fastballs that met the intersection of home plate dirt and infield grass at belt level and arrive at the catcher's mitt beside the hitter's letters. Batters could never adequately adjust to the sudden arc on the ball even if they knew Gibson's style. Hypothetically, they could make their cut letters-high, but the arch's angle changed from pitch to pitch according to the speed of the ball in a way it was thrown. When Gibson's pitches started sailing from the mound, he had a near foolproof way of sending any batter back to the dugout talking to himself.

Nolan Ryan is a superb fastball pitcher, but it is usually difficult for an umpire to call balls and strikes behind the plate because he was such a chronic complainer. He had a difficult time understanding that pitchers could not throw *and* determine the count on the batter. Most National League umpires just wished Nolan would cut the officiating routine and leave the judgment calls to the sport's paid judges.

Jim Maloney of the New York Mets was a great fastball pitcher who never seems to get the fanfare he deserved. Jim had the speed and control, but the defense of the Mets in those days was nearly as porous as a screen door. If he had settled into a starting position with the Cardinals or Dodgers, I'm sure the historic baseball compendium would reflect an entirely different set of stats for his career.

The fastest hurler I've ever had the pleasure and danger of umpiring was Steve Dalkowski in the Carolina League. During the mid-Fifties, he was throwing an early, unnamed prototype of the Harpoon missile for the Baltimore Orioles organization in Wilson, North Carolina. Dalkowski had the great psychological advantage of throwing fastballs that scared batters out of their pinstripes. Guys would take three quick swings just to live for the next game. The guy could rocket the ball with startling speed but he usually had absolutely no idea on what or whom it would land. One amazing pitch zoomed past the batter, was a blur beside the catcher, and was fleeting memory as it flew past me into and through the backstop screen and finally came to rest somewhere in the stadium parking lot.

The forkball is a relatively new addition to the big-league pitching menu and it is perhaps the least understood pitch in the hurler's retinue. The forker is held with index and middle fingers separated but extended. It drops like a sinker as it approaches the plate, but unlike the age-old sinker, it arrives with a backspin that causes it to lose its speed. The batter sees the ball approach at a certain speed and is confused as it reaches his hitting zone because it suddenly loses momentum. The simultaneous drop of the forkball and its decrease in speed tends to create an optical illusion that is difficult for all three people around the home plate to follow.

Not many pitchers include the forkball in their diet, fewer still become masters. Elroy Face of the Pirates and Bruce Sutter or of the Cubs, Cards, and Braves were real forker's (and good pitchers, too).

There is an excellent reason why people who live their lives with only one oar in the water are called screwballs. The pitch is completely crazy. It is thrown with a reverse spin and breaks in the opposite direction from a curveball. Nearly every pitcher who has ever signed a major-league contract can at least approximate something resembling a curveball. The screwball requires a more complex, opposite wrist movement from the curve in the release process. While a right-hander throws a curve that breaks to his left and conversely for the southpaw, the screwball arches slightly to the opposite direction of the throwing arm while in flight and then suddenly curves in the direction of the pitcher's throwing arm. This can be a devastatingly effective pitch if it's breaking properly, especially for the southpaw. It is a difficult pitch for an umpire to call for the same reasons it is hard for the batter to hit – it breaks in the opposite direction from the more commonplace curve. When a good pitcher can juxtapose his routine between screwballs and curves, the batter usually has a serious problem with his sense of direction. Just before it reaches the plate, the ball can go in either direction. Umpires have to take the time to deliberately follow each pitch as it crosses the plate. Tug McGraw and Mike Marshall were two of the best screwballers on and off the field during my years in the majors.

Knuckleballers are the villains of the pitching staffs. Instead of deceiving matters with slick pitches that challenge their timing or confuse their sense of direction, the knuckler rides like a little zeppelin on the park's airwaves. It has the audacity not to take a flight of its own, but hijacks a trip atop the prevalent airstreams. The knuckleball artist does not cause the pitch to sink, curve, or slight, he only knows how to release it to the guiding hands of Mother Nature. Even the most adept knuckleheads cannot predict where their unruly throws will eventually meet the catcher's mitt. Like snowflakes, no two knuckleballs will ever be the same, even if they're aimed. Pitchers unskilled in throwing the knuckler quickly discover that the ball can be master of the man. Without the special grip and release the ball can seem to have a mind of its own. The real expert has enough mastery so that he can make the ball reach the bottom half of the strike zone.

Knuckleballs are perhaps the most physically economical kind of throw a pitcher can make. It does not demand a rifle arm and great speed. Masters like Phil Niekro, Hoyt Wilhelm, and Charley Huff were able to extend their careers by expending the least amount of energy per strike – all thanks to the bumpy ride of the knuckleball.

Ron Luciano has claimed that it takes four or five, complete seasons to adequately call balls and strikes for a good knucklehead. Don't believe it! Chances are good that enough of experience with knucklers in the minors will at least give a major league rookie a rough schematic of how they operate in the majors. If the umpire knows a knuckler is bobbing and weaving along the stadium airwaves, he has to be particularly patient, watch the complete run of each pitch and not make a rush to judgment. His primary problem is not to get into the mode of anticipating the most likely place where the knuckleball will actually first cross the plate, but take an extra second to determine exactly where it made his rendezvous with the plate.

It's been claimed that when a passing quarterback, or a control pitcher, or an expert dart thrower and even a champion bowler suddenly has to concentrate on aiming the tool of his trade, he loses poise and self-confidence. Psychologically it seems that a control pitcher can best manipulate his pitches when he naturally throws the ball instead of consciously working on the control aspect of his art. Good control pitchers naturally pitch with the guiding element of control. No one has to whisper the suggestion in their ear that the strike zone is their prime concern.

Unfortunately, control experts play a hide and seek game with the early showers. If they're making the strike zone, control pitchers are the most ecstatic breed of pitchers there can be on the mound. But when they're bad, they're very bad. As the hits become more frequent and more costly, the controller begins to think he can regain his forte by straining to aim the ball. When he must place the ball for exact position instead of naturally throwing, most pitching coaches will nudge their managers to deliver the sad news.

Many controllers have no special accent on the ball except for their uncanny ability to position it in various parts of the strike zone. They may not have a very fast pitch in their repertoire or even a decent curveball, sinker, or change-up. Usually their hopes rest in naturally placing a ball at the level just across one of the corners of the plate.

Cal MacLish of the Phillies was a real master of plate control. He'd keep batters off balance by alternating between balls and perfect strikes. Once he raised the ante to a 2-2 or full count, the batter began to have high hopes of drawing a walk. Then he nicely placed a low strike over the plate and send the man back to the dugout talking to himself.

The brush back pitch is one of the mound's strongest non-verbal means of communication with the plate. Most of the time, it is the pitcher's subtle way of saying, "Stand back, I own some of the plate's real estate, too!!"

Batters will sometimes hug the home plate to attain an edge on outside pitches. If one man parked a ball over the outfield wall, the pitcher may think that the act can be duplicated by the next batter. The successor in the batter's box may be informed that he is hedging in too close for the pitcher's comfort. Brush back balls assert the pitcher's right of the plate and make a delicate psychological point that he is still throwing a hardball at great speed just inches away from the batter. It's a legal throw and most hitters and umpires understand its import.

The very worst thing a pitcher can possibly do on the mound is throw at a batter. There is no good reason for a bean ball pitch and absolutely no reason for a bean ball pitcher to be tolerated in the sport. Not only is the pitcher who attempts to low-bridge a man malicious, he violates a major unspoken code of the sport. The batter that is hit in the head is never quite the same player ever again. The risk of permanent physical injury is the primary but by no means the sole concern he'll have to face. Even if a player is hit in the head without any physical repercussions, psychologically he will never return to the plate as the same hitter he once was. A gnawing feeling of discomfort battles for his concentration at the plate. He wonders if the next pitch may catch him again and cause permanent injury. Even a player that acts seemingly undaunted by the incident will show telltale psychological signs of being ill at ease at bat. He'll over-react to a brush back pitch by hurling himself outside the batter's box or become less aggressive with his bat and wait a costly fraction of a second before trying to meet the ball. The art of hitting is difficult enough to master under circumstances of complete concentration. If a player must share his potential hitting prowess with an uncomfortable psychological undertow, trips to the plate usually become frustrating and lonely experiences.

During my time behind the plate I've seen Joe Coleman hit square in the face by a ball aimed to hurt him. Bob Abodaca of the Mets was knocked in the head by a pitch that seem to me to be purposefully targeted for him. Neither man was ever quite the same player again. Sadly enough, the low-bridge pitch is the

189

most expedient and malicious way of cutting-short of promising career.

Players and umpires seem to acquire a sixth sense in regard to the bean ball. As soon as the pitch is completed, both parties seem to instinctively know if it was a very close brush back, and honest wild pitch, or one aimed to hit the batter. The matter is an almost inherent, "knee-jerk" reaction and doesn't seem to require any further clarification. Baseball fans anywhere can recall incidents when batters have dropped out of reflex and then charged the mound out of reflex because a sixth sense instinctively informed them that the pitch was designed to hurt them.

Because there is no means of probing a pitcher's mind, there is no conclusive means of establishing evidence to ban the low-bridger. An umpire and a batter may "know" a particular pitcher intentionally hurled a bean ball, but the league offices need more than healthy subjective judgments. Home

CHAPTER EIGHT

THE OFFICIALS OF BASEBALL

"I don't think he had a shy bone in his body." – Fred Pryor, speaking of his father

During my 20 years in the major leagues, I don't think there was ever a time I could have been accused of being an "office man." I was a big, well-tanned, crew cut field man – an incorrigible baseball tramp who was accustomed to the wind, sun, and sometimes the rain of the game. While some umpires made periodic pilgrimages to the league president's office for a petty grievance of one kind or another – I was somewhere on the road, performing the city to city shuffle in big league heaven. I was strictly a member of the lunch pail crowd – proud that my shirttails blew in the wind far away from the machinations of league politics. I knew I did my job well and didn't need the League president to tell me so.

In all my years with the National League, I must have graced the president's office an entire five times. Those were only mandatory occasions when I was called to a meeting for one reason or another. Evidently, the league president did miss me and I didn't especially miss him. We performed our jobs separately and distinctly from one another and somehow 162 games were played and the National Pastime chugged onward.

God is very high in Heaven and for an umpire, the Commissioner of Baseball and his two league presidents are very high too. The umpire is not only the representative of both the commissioner and league president each time he emerges from the locker room onto the field, but he is baseball's officialdom while he is working. The umpire upholds and enforces the tradition, rules, and regulations of the game of baseball on the playing field. Major league umpires take this responsibility seriously, but there is precious little support from either the commissioner or league president for his efforts.

Warren Giles bought my American Association contract and resurrected me from the doldrums of the minors to become a major leaguer. He took a curious interest in my well-being. He was a thorough, efficient executive who upheld an arm's distance between his office and his employees. But Giles could let his hair hang down on occasions. If he happened to be in a National League city for a game, he made a point of meeting and talking to us for about 15 minutes before a game. Giles would take an umpiring crew to dinner once in a while and involve himself in a little small talk with his troops. Giles was crisp, clear, occasionally an over-executive, but he had a few warm chinks in his official armor. He was still capable of unbuttoning his collar and talking shop with his boys – the National League umpires.

"Chub" Feeney clipped his collar tighter and turned his ear away from the umpires. I felt that while Chub cared as much about baseball as any league president in the history of the sport, he could not have cared less about his boys in the trenches. He never asked the Giles' questions of "How's the wife and kids?" or "How's the family?" Chub never even knew we had families. He recognize our faces from the stadium programs, but any familiarity ended then and there.

Umpiring crews who were working hundreds of miles from homes and loved ones – guys who had umpired the sport they loved and dedicated their lives to, were never invited by Chub to share a taco lunch. Giles' fifteen minute sessions with umpires before a game were whittled to maybe five minutes with Chub. If he called the meeting, it was a puny three-minute rush session. He was a very busy man and didn't have time for his boys – "his umpires." An umpire could easily begin to wonder if he didn't have time to talk with his own umpires, then who does he have time for hour after hour, day after day?

Umpires are delegated to uphold the rules and regs of baseball, but it's a sad commentary when they're told to be policemen on the field and discover the league presidents will not support their decisions. Fine a ballplayer for ugly, punk language that would make a drill sergeant blush and then have the league president flippantly reversed the umpire's on-the-field call only serves to belittle the greatness of the sport. The hierarchy of baseball needs big, two-hearted officials who won't knuckle under to the whims of million-dollar bonus babies and come to the defense of the real intentions of the game.

In recent baseball history, the league presidents have been elevated from the ranks of the general managers. Until the time they assumed the league office, it was their business to understand and know players. Their stock-in-trade involved making the right deals, trades, purchases, and player transactions that built a ball club from the front office downwards. The GM is administrator, architect, personnel director, chief scout, financial coordinator, main bottle washer and soothsayer for the franchise. But a general manager's special familiarity with players can often leave him vulnerable to understanding other facets of the sport. Umpires tend to become nothing more than official, but necessary footnotes in their eyes.

Warren Giles, Chub Feeney, and Lee MacPhail were general managers long before they became league presidents. Frequently the league presidents reverse an umpire's request for a fine or other punitive actions against a player. Often times, they've known the players in question much longer and on a much more intimate basis than their own umpires – particularly if they were on the roster of the team the president once ran. It's a tough pill for an umpire to swallow when he nabs a player for outrageous language or actions and then discovers by a "personal "telegram that the entire situation has been dismissed by the league president. So much for being told by the sport's high officials that umpires should also be cops on the field.

Sometimes the league presidents border on downright hostility toward umpires. During the 1979 umpires' strike, National League president Chub Feeney declared that it wasn't such a bad thing the boys in blue weren't showing up for work. He claimed he could get umpires from just about any street corner. In the power clashes between owners and owners, owners and big-ticket players, owners and the players' union, owners and the commissioner, the umpires are like the shrimp caught between a collision of whales.

Recent commissioners of baseball exert themselves only on rare occasions to make a few but far between exhibitions to meet the umpires. There are less than 52 umpires in major league baseball. It's not a taxing task for the commissioner, or especially a league president to know each umpire on an individual basis – that is, if he really wanted to. Commissioners Judge Landis and Happy Chandler knew their umpires and consulted them about many field issues. A visit to the umpires' locker room, a sincere hello, a vote of thanks now and then, and a display of support can go a long way for the umpires directly, but also indirectly for the fans, the players, and the sport in general.

Before an Astros game in Houston, Bowie Kuhn decided to make an exemplary and extraordinary call on the umpires' locker room. He was in the company of a Texas state senator and took particular delight in the high esteem and good graces of his guests. Bowie walked into the locker room and proudly announced, "These are my boys!" I remember my fellow umpires being more surprised by his visit then impressed.

After a round of gentlemanly acknowledgments, the state senator and Bowie Kuhn were prepared to leave. I thought it was a phony visit. It was just an instinctive call. He didn't have any of the umpires' well-being in mind. Bowie was on an express course to impress this Texas state senator with being able to fling open the umpires' locker room door unannounced and suddenly become "The Commissioner" for the moment. I couldn't resist making a comment to Bowie and his legislator buddy.

"It's good to see you, Commissioner. We don't get a chance to see you that often." After Bowie and the senator left the locker room, the rest of the crew wanted to know why in the hell I made such a tainted remark. My heart had just blurted out instead of my head. Home

CHAPTER NINE

MISCELLANEOUS COMMENTARY

"I never went to umpires' school so they assigned me to work in Puerto Rico for several winter league seasons to gain experience. And what an experience it was!" –Paul Pryor

Early New York Mets

Anyone caring to carefully analyze the early Mets should be equipped with a good sense of humor. The Stengel teams were stocked with some of baseball's real characters that just happened to have big hearts and puny bats. The Mets were one of the early expansion clubs and filled their roster with other big league players. The problem, however, was that these players were more than frequently the twentieth, the twenty-second, or twenty-fifth players from other big league rosters. There were more refugees from other teams that drifted into the dugout in those years than had scuttled into Ellis Island.

"Marvelous Marv" Thornberry played first base and got a big kick out of stepping into the batter's box and swinging at the ball. Don "Popeye" Zimmer rolled around over at third base. In the autumn of his career, Richie Ashburn left the Phillies to play centerfield for Casey Stengel. Choo-Choo Coleman caught the pitches and had a good time shooting the breeze with batters and umpires. Scientifically, these guys were not exactly the nucleus of a great team, they were more like the electrons that are lost in one chemical process and picked up by another. They had to go somewhere, so they came to the Mets.

The Designated Hitter

The "Designated Hitter" does not play a big part in the vocabulary of many National League umpires. Innovations like the faster ball, Astroturf, and free agency have permeated both leagues. But the advent of the designated hitter belongs exclusively to the American League.

I'm convinced that the designated hitter is like a drink from the Fountain of Youth for many older sluggers. It has prolonged the active careers of a number of great hitters who would have been considered too old to hop around with the kids in the field. Some older players still have the timing, swing, and hitting judgment to maintain a good batting average and slugging percentage but have lost the edge of speed and the agility to effectively operate in the field. Some great hitters are allowed to continue as great hitters long after the fleet has abandoned their feet. Players like Carl Yastrzemski, Rico Carty, and Orlando Cepeda remained valuable assets at the plate at a time when they could have had trouble chasing hits off the walls.

Designated hitting has also lessened some of the strategic aspects of the game. A pitcher can act brazen on the mound without ever having to receive a dose of his own medicine. Pitchers can brush batters back from the plate, throw to scare, even throw to hit the man at bat without having to face the same treatment.

The "Balloon" Protector

Until the 1960s, American League umpires behind the plate were still required to wear "the balloon." This is the cumbersome, mattress-like protector that is fit through the shoulder and protects those members of my trade who do want untimely excursions to the hospital. It is also the device that was responsible for making most umpires look like giant box turtles on the field.

I've always believed that umpires not only have to be thick skinned characters in their own right, but should be dressed to handle the foibles of outrageous pitches. The balloon provided adequate protection, but it left a lot to be desired for maneuverability.

I was calling pitches once in an American Association game when former National League Pres. Warren Giles happened to be in the stands. My balloon had recently broken and I was outfitted for the game with an inside chest protector. Without the added bulk of the balloon, my usual gestures for indicating a strike seemed very frightening.

My style for calling a strike involved turning my body to the side and emphatically clinching two raised fists. It seemed a clear enough gesture for all parties, and I had been using it for years. While fans certainly knew a strike was called, there were times the players gave me a second or third glance as I stood with my fist raised while they trailed their bats behind them to the dugouts. Without a balloon and with both fists raised. I must have cut a profile like Jack Dempsey behind the plate.

After watching nine innings of this pugilistic demonstration behind the plate, Mr. Giles called me over to his seat after the game. "Kid," he said "you call the great game. But who are you fighting out there, anyways? Those players are going to think you want to fight them."

Now umpires are allowed to use either the inside chest protector or the balloon, depending upon their individual preferences. This is become a great equalizing device between the National and American Leagues. When American League umpires were required to wear the balloon, they usually had to look over the head of the catcher to watch the incoming pitches. This had the tendency to alter the view so that a low pitch tended to look slightly higher than it really was. Conversely, the National League umpires had the reputation of being in the low strike league. Without the obstruction of the balloon, we could position ourselves lower and look for the outside pitch with right-handed batters.

Umpire Schooling

Schooling has become a necessary credential for virtually any aspiring umpire hoping to enter the ranks of professional baseball. The days of barnstorming umpires preaching the minor leagues, let alone the majors, but putting their time on the way up the hawse pipe are over. What Sputnik did to change American education – big-money players, TV rights, free agency, and the growing complexities of the game have helped change the credentials umpires forever.

The Joe Brinkman and Harry Wendelstedt Schools attract not only the guys that want a career in the pros, but sports enthusiasts and women who want to thoroughly know the rules of baseball. Graduation from either school is bound to make someone better umpire what they are planning to officiate high school games or enter the professional ranks. Both schools give a complete course in the mechanics and fundamentals of the sport. Nearly every play in the rulebook is gone over and over again. They learn the right way to call balls and strikes, where to position themselves for play calling, and finish knowing the rulebook better than Moses knew the Bible.

But what can't be taught on the school fields of Florida are the necessary human ingredients of umpiring. Common sense and good judgment are instinctive qualities that are part and parcel to making a good umpire. A fledging umpire they realize that he will be blitzkrieged on the field by an irate manager, but until that first manager charges onto the field and recites retinue of expletive deleted and dangling participles that would embarrass a platoon Marines on their first liberty – then he'll have to think fast on his feet. An umpire has to be able to listen to beefs on the field, know when to turn volcanic managers off, listen to tirades about your family ancestry and know when to shut it all off, protect themselves from the slings and arrows of verbal abuse and retain the dignity of the sport and continue the game – sometimes all at once.

American League Colleagues

An umpire is so immersed in his travel schedule, players, managers, and politics within his league that he can scarcely get a close look at life in the other league. As a National League umpire, I only encountered my American League counterparts

201

during a once-a-year umpires' conference or a happenstance meeting on the field during a World Series or All-Star game.

My knowledge of the American league players made them as much of an anomaly to me as they were to the fans in general. But I discovered how one great American League player knew all about me and conveyed his unique respect for Paul Pryor on the field.

During a game in the 1980 World Series between the Phillies and the Royals when I was calling balls and strikes behind the plate, George Brett stepped into the batter's box and an interesting conversation ensued.

Bob Boone was catching for the Phillies and took a particular interest in George's bout with hemorrhoids. "Hey, George, how are those hemorrhoids?" he asked. His bedside manner was just a little abrupt.

"Very disturbing," Brent replied matter-of-factly.

George thought about what he had just said and turned around to me. "Well, Paul Pryor, my favorite umpire." It tickled the cockles of my umpire's heart.

Bob Boone, like most players, could not understand how or why an American League player would shed such terrible graces on an umpire in another league. Boone naturally knew the umpires is his league were a brood of lazy, slovenly, sloth-like ingrates. So the next time Brett came to bat, Bob Boone decided to investigate this natural phenomenon.

"How can Pryor be your favorite umpire?" Boone asked him. I watch him on TV to see what the strike zone looks like," Brent claimed.

Sometimes it's *very disturbing* to see what a player will resort to when he thinks he might be the butt-end of talk in the umpires' locker room.

Stan Musial

Stan Musial is one of the greatest ballplayers in the history of the sport. Not only was he in achiever *par excellence* on the field, but he was a great competitor, a talented player, a humanitarian, and a great human being.

Stan "The Man" Musial used to pass me on the field and always had an upbeat word to say. No matter what the score was in the bottom of the ninth inning, Musial would trot pass me and ask, "How you doing? Everything all right, umps?" And he meant what he asked.

I was calling balls and strikes behind the plate one day in the old Polo Grounds when the St. Louis Cardinals played the Mets. Stan wacked out three solid homeruns in that game and came up to bat for a fourth time when I called him out on a half swing.

Cardinals' manager Johnny Keane had absolutely no sense of humor about the call. I knew Stan broke his wrist in going for the ball and I instinctively thought that Stan knew full well he broke his wrist in anticipation of swinging. But Johnny Keene was hoping for a measly win against the Mets and a new single-game home run record for Stan.

The next day I was working third base when Stan jogged past me on his way to the outfield. As he passed me he said, "You know that guy sure fooled me on that pitch." Hallelujah for irate umpires.

Bill Jackowski

Once Bill Jackowski was working the right field foul line when he called Bobby Bragan of the Braves out on a close play at third. Bragan swore up and down and up again that he was safe, but Bill stood his umpire's ground. He had to lurch back at Jackowski with something. He felt caught between a base and a hard place and in a fit of blind frustration he read Jackowski "down country".

Most baseball people in the National League new Bill was a devoted Catholic. In a game predominated by heathens, he was definitely considered a religious man. Bragan took a cheap shot at Bill's faith and told him on his trip back to the dugout "go say a rosary".

Jackowski was taken aback by the comment and felt hurt that a player would stoop so low as to belittle his religion. He decided to protest Bragan's comment and he notified Warren Giles, the National League President and requested a hearing in his offices in Cincinnati. Ed Sudol and John Kibler were witnesses to the incident and accompanied Ed to Mr. Giles' offices. Certainly in a case like this the National League would support an umpire and take some punitive measures. The presiding opinion among the umpires was that Bragan would be suspended or at least fined. Wrong.

Mr. Giles listened attentively to the umpires' account of the ordeal and decided the most prudent course of action was to do absolutely nothing. Virtually any verbal transgression against an umpire can be made without punitive actions from the league offices. A player can have a verbal field day with an umpire and not be punished. Today, the prima donna players are kings of the diamond. While umpires are nominally delegated to enforce the rules of baseball on the field, they have been made into paper tigers by league management.

George Steinbrenner

George Steinbrenner loves to step before the microphones and take swings at umpires. But the problem with the Yankee owner is that he too often swings without a bat on a field that is only in his imagination.

For 162 games a year, George has little or nothing to say about the umpires. When the Yankees lose a World Series game, his teams poor hitting, poor pitching, and poor fielding or the opponents' good hitting, good fielding, and good pitching are never responsible for his team's loss. The National League umpires have now conspired to beat the Yankees on the field.

I think George is distressed that while he has all the money in Tampa, Florida and the South Bronx, the integrity of baseball on the field is still under the control of the umpires. That's something that can't be bought, borrowed, or mortgaged and George misses the control.

During the 1977 World Series between the Dodgers can't Yankees, George was perturbed over the playing of his Bronx Bombers and blamed the National League umpire delegation for some of the Yankee shortcomings. The National League boys, he claimed, bent over backwards to help *their* team in the series.

John McSherry had home plate duty for one game of that series and was fitted with a microphone. Late in the game, Dodger manager Tommy Lasorda went to the mound to make a pitching change. McSherry waited the customer period of time and walked to the pitching mound.

John asked Lasorda if he was now going to bring in relief from the bullpen.

Half-jokingly and in a manner that only a major league manager uses, he told McSherry, "I don't know. What would you do?"

John told him simply to do whatever had to be done in this situation. Period.

Lasorda told him that if he could stay another ten seconds that he'd make the change right then and there.

Steinbrenner heard the conversation between McSherry and Lasorda and went through the roof of the House that Ruth Built. He recognized the discussion to be a clear-cut example of how the National League umpires sacrifice their integrity to help the National League team.

Joe Garagiola

Before a Braves game once in Atlanta, Joe Garagiola and several of his friends made an unexpected visit to the umpires' locker room. Apparently Joe and his pals had been talking about how umpires behind the plate discriminate between the hitting stars and the poorer batters when they called balls and strikes. The conversation that began outside the locker room was carried inside for our benefit.

Garagiola informed his friends in front of us that hitters the caliber of Hank Aaron were constantly being helped by umpires. The boys in blue bent over backwards to assist players like Aaron and even the .300 plus hitters when they're at bat. They more than usually get any benefit of the doubt with the strike zone because it has a tendency to suddenly expand when they're in the batters' box. The .200 hitters will get called out on strikes after watching highballs, low balls, and inside pitches pass them by.

I never knew if Joe attributed his own batting success to umpires or whether he thought Hank Aaron was helped to be an all-time baseball great because umpires liked great hitters. But Garagiola evidently didn't realize he had instantly changed the umpires' dressing room into a lions' den as he merrily continued philosophizing away. This was tantamount to paying a call on a College of Cardinals meeting just to preach heresy.

World Series Comments

World Series are much more than just the season's final contest between the best teams of each league. It is baseball's crowning ceremony, a time when the sport's fanfare and panache are on festive display. The host cities become more vibrant at World Series time. People who are not even fans take the time to pay attention to the baseball season's grand finale. Radios and portable televisions suddenly find their way into schools and workplaces. It is a sport's yearly benchmark, the net result of the thousands of games played in the spring and summer. The action is recorded in the minds of millions of fans so that in hindsight the blur of some distant season and all its faces and plays and nuances are somehow recalled by the winner and loser in the World Series.

Everything about a series seems more vivid, more spectacular. It is a time when little boys finish rehearsing the swings of their heroes until the players return after six long months to the ballparks in April. Baseball talk enters the course of more conversations than any other time of the season.

No stadium looks quite as exciting as when it hosts the Series. Red, white, and blue festoons are draped from the rooftops; colorful pennants and flags roll in the breeze. Even the Astroturf seems greener and more luxuriant. And for a week in the early fall an American tradition renews itself.

While playing in a World Series is among any player's greatest aspirations, becoming one of its stars is among the sport's greatest experiences. Events have a unique way of magnifying themselves above and beyond the feats in 162 games in a season. A home run not only seizes the moment but seems to become a great picture in a historic panoply of the sport's great moments.

Umpires have the same feelings about World Series as big leaguers. Officiating a series is as much a hallmark of achievement and success as it is for the players. It was a thrill for me to umpire every game during the course of the long season, but umpiring in a World Series is in a privileged category all its own.

The Brooklyn Dodgers

A number of baseball writers and sports columnist claimed that the Brooklyn Dodgers' move from Ebbets Field to Los Angeles was an irretrievable loss to the sport. It seemed to substantiate the notion that despite the colorful history, great attendance and fantastic support from loyal fans, an owner could capriciously yank a team away from his cultural roots and resettle it on a whim to the other side of the nation. Ebbets Field and the Dodgers were as firmly integrated in the whole life of Brooklyn as Coney Island, Prospect Park, and Flatbush Avenue. Brooklyn has never been the same since the Boys of Summer left and, I suppose, in many ways, the Dodgers had never been the same either.

Brooklyn was devastated when the Dodgers left town. The team had woven itself through the cultural and social fabric of the entire borough. An amalgamation of people who had only a half generation or generation earlier greeted their new land at Ellis Island found common ground with older Brooklynites at Ebbets Field. To pull the team out of New York right in front of millions of disbelieving fans seems to substantiate the belief that fans, support, nostalgia, and history meant nothing. All that could be altered forever by the decision of the team's owner and no one could do anything about it.

Many Brooklyn Dodger fans lost interest in the sport after 1957. Some joined ranks and found cause to root for the new National League Mets several years later. Most could not move their loyalties across town to the Bronx and the Yankees – that was complete anathema. Few die-hard Ebbets Field Dodger fans saw it fit to follow their old team in the newspapers and on television while they played in a strange, far-off city that had little in common with the streets of Brooklyn.

I've always had strong sentiments about the Dodgers move from New York to Los Angeles, but my twenty years in the majors have convinced me that the O'Malley family made the right move.

Until 1958, St. Louis was geographically furthest city west to host the major league team. The city that hugged the western shore of the Mississippi River was barely the Gateway city to the West. A whole other world within the United States had shared only vicariously in the American Pastime. From San Diego to Seattle, and Dallas to Kansas City, a vibrant wide-open territory needed to be addressed. They had passively always looked to the East at a sport that had decades and decades earlier captured the interest and imagination of millions of Americans – both east and west of the Big Muddy.

Respect

When Aretha Franklin sings about R-E-S-P-E-C-T and Rodney Dangerfield jokes about it, I think they must have professional umpires in mind. There's so little of it around for umpires these days that they probably wouldn't know what to do with it if it ever happened to hit them in the face. Fans will always shortchange an umpire. That's a simple fact of baseball life that will never change. They largely regard umpires as bums. We're the guys that never really got out in the real world for an honest day's work. But the fans' sensibilities really do not affect an umpire's job in the field. The lack of respect shown by players, managers, coaches, front office people, and the league personnel *does* affect the umpires' ability to function on the field – and this is the most unkind cut of all.

Umpires are directed at special league meetings to pay particular attention to illegal pitches, actor balls, bean ball pitchers, balks, etc. But when we perform our jobs and report these incidents to the league's' officials, no one is willing to back us up.

Records

There is sound logic to the notion that records are meant to be broken. They are the benchmarks that create a kind of artificial ceiling for players to jump through. But a broken record is normally held and suspect. Somehow there is a certain sense of security and revering the great players of by-gone years. Many fans feel secure with the tried and true images of their old baseball heroes – a newcomer to those ranks frequently finds it difficult for the sport to automatically accept his records. Some fans look at Pete Rose's all-time hit record and feel obliged to examine it in light of Ty Cobb's career. Antagonists are quick to point out the facts that Cobb did not play with teams in the National League, and that he accomplished the record by playing fewer seasons with fewer games and reached his record at an earlier age. But the more discerning fans should realize that imposed stumbling blocks of age, number of games per season, the number of teams in a league, etc., are facts completely beyond Pete Rose's control.

He had no say or control over determining the number of games this season, nor the fact that baseball expanded its number of franchises. Rose's only problem was that he played the same game as Ty Cobb, but played two generations later.

I've always thought that a player should break a record during the course of his day-to-day appearances on the field. A lot of players like to break a record before their hometown fans. Sore thumbs and pulled muscles too often seem to debilitate players on the road when they are only a steal, a strikeout, or a hit away from breaking a record. I've always aligned myself with the conviction that baseball requires a daily commitment of 100%. Goldbricking on the road to reach a milestone at home – in front of cheering fans, exploding graphics on the scoreboard and fireworks is completely understandable. But I maintain the old-fashioned notion that each game should be treated as a challenge and the desire for each player to give his best should be a foregone conclusion.

Hank Aaron

Everything good fans have heard about Hank Aaron is true. His career can be encapsuled in a five-letter word – G-R-E-A-T – and perhaps a little more. Number 44 of the Braves could throw, hit, steal bases – all in a quiet, gentle, great style. Hank was a pleasure to see at work on the field. His only shortcoming was that he was never a publicity seeker. But in light of such an illustrious career, he is perhaps the most underrated and on acclaimed hero in the history of baseball.

Ruth's career home run record withstood a durable litmus test in time. It was a feat thought to be etched in stone. A mild-mannered player from a great metropolitan team who preferred a session of quiet batting practice to the riotous circumstances of marathon journalistic sessions was not considered by many to be made of the same stuff as heroes. While lesser talented players gloated in the footlights of cursory victories and milestones, Aaron plodded on and on and on and silently amassed baseball's career home runs record under the very noses of the sport's journalists. Unfortunately, they never recognized a diamond when it was in their hands.

Pete Rose

Pete Rose had been barreling along base paths long enough most fans and players have become used to most of the nuances of his running style. For example, "Charley Hustle" customarily reacts to a clear-cut single by charging around first base and then adroitly reaching a screeching halt. The position of his hit lets him know that he has an easy single but throughout ninety feet between home plate and first he's thinking second base. Once he rounds first and determines he cannot safely advance further, Pete comes to a feet grinding stop. While the defense is returning the ball to the pitcher, Pete mozies back to first. This is one of the few occasions he ever moves slowly on the field. But his way of charging around first, applying his brakes, and then the slow sauntered back to the bag is so routine that it looks like an instant replay run over and over again.

Pete's first base choreography is so well known by friend and foe alike that in one game at Veterans' Stadium, his old Cincinnati teammates pulled a fast one on him. I had the first base assignment in a game between the Phillies and the Reds. During the game, Pete had a single and performed his traditional maneuver of rounding first for a cleat-wrenching halt before meandering back to the back. But Dave Conception anticipated Pete's actions and threw to teammate Danny Driesen on first.

Before Pete could react, Driesen positioned himself with one foot on the base while he held the ball to make a tag. Pete tried to run around his old teammate to reach the bag and I called him out for trying to run around Driesen to the base.

He had absolutely no sense of humor about my call. Phillies manager Dallas Green charged out of the dugout while 40,000 screaming fans were ready to hang me by my thumbs from Independence Hall.

In the top of the ninth inning Pete jogged out to me by first base and said, "Hey, Paul, I didn't even know about that rule."

"How about getting on the microphone and telling the fans that you didn't know about the rule and that Paul Pryor was right in this call?" I asked him.

Pete just smiled at that suggestion and went about his business of playing first base. There was a look on his face that connoted his thoughts – not in front of 40,000 fans I won't. Thanks for the offer, but the monkey likes it better on the umpire's back anyway.

Roberto Clemente

I once called Pittsburgh Pirate great Roberto Clemente out on strikes. He apparently didn't agree with my call and responded with a stream of invective in Spanish. To his surprise, I was able to answer him back, *in Spanish!* Here's what I said; "Estudie Espanol en la escula la para dos annos. Para afuera!" (Translation: "I studied Spanish in school for two years. Take a hike!")

Clemente then went back to the Pirates' bench and warned all the other Latin players to be careful what they said to me because that I could speak Spanish!

The 1979 Umpires' Strike

Most people have little or no understanding of the background of the 1979 umpires' strike. It was chalked up as yet another escapade of baseball's personnel demanding an exorbitant amount of money to participate in a little boys' game.

For six months of the year umpires can lead somewhat "normal" family lives. For the other six months of the baseball season they lead a strange, dual life on the road. Umpires receive a straight salary and a per diem allotment. The latter comprises the wherewithal to pay for taxis to and from the airport, to and from the ballparks and hotels, restaurants, tips, hotels, laundry, dry cleaning, etc., etc., etc.

The strike of 1979 was an effort to increase our salaries in order to more adequately cope with the everyday expenses of living on the road. Players, coaches, and managers make the grand, imperial six month excursion of each season on the road, but their ball clubs take care of the day-to-day accommodations, transportation, and meals. This is not the case for umpires. Our salary was one item, the per diem encumbrances of each day away from home was another altogether. The strike tried to increase the umpires' salaries in order to handle costly expedition of shuffling from city to city during the season.

When Nature Calls...

Players will have the good fortune of being able to answer Nature's calling in the dugout bathrooms between innings. Umpires are not really afforded this luxury. While the players have easy access to such facilities, umpires have to escape from the field and walk to somewhere in the interior of the stadium to their dressing room. With the exception of the more modern stadiums, the umpires' bathrooms are abominations plumbing back to the Middle Ages.

It does not appear professional for an umpire to make frequent excursions to the bathroom. Players, coaches, managers, fans are quickly apt to feel that the umpire's mind is preoccupied with dire bodily urges instead of the game. The dugout is also a sacred domain of the players. Umpires are frequently unwelcome strangers to the players' abode. I cringe at the thought of even considering walking into a home team's dugout with Leo Durocher to use his team's bathroom after I threatened to throw him out of the game minutes earlier.

Drinking liquids before a game is an umpiring taboo. Standing on the field for nine innings has the precarious effect of making fluids follow the natural course of gravity. When American League umpires are assigned home plate duty in Royals Stadium, the constant flush of the outfield waterfall has a tendency to give the batter some strange illusions. I'm surprised Royals' owner Ewing Kaufman has not been asked by the American League to install a Port O' Potty near one of the dugouts.

I was umpiring first base at Pittsburgh in 1965 when I had to respond to an urgent call from Mother Nature. It was the fifth inning break and I walked to the Pirates' dugout and asked to use the bathroom. Willie Stargell emerged from the bathroom just as I was preparing to enter. I got through the threshold of the Pirates bathroom when Willie playfully slammed the door behind him. The lock snapped and I was trapped in the bathroom.

I roared and pounded on the door to no avail. Everyone else in the stadium was watching the game. Finally some sympathetic Pirate heard my screaming and sent for the grounds crew. In order to liberate me from the bathroom, the maintenance men had to remove the hinges from the door. Each turn of the screwdriver seemed like an eternity. I suspected that the Pirates may have heard my pounding and screams and decided to let me live with my claustrophobia. Besides, as far as they were concerned one less umpire field was just fine. Fortunately, my partner on second base positioned himself between first and second to cover both bases on the grounds crew work to free me from the john.

A half inning later the door was removed and I pranced onto the field again. The Pirate coaches kept asking me if I had a case of diarrhea. Willie Stargell sat in one corner of the dugout with his hand cupped over his mouth giggling.

I think he was convinced that he'd never see me honestly call a pitch on him again. I'm going to become a garbologist, and quit baseball, he said, as he chuckled in embarrassment. Home

CHAPTER TEN

"WHAT WAS IT LIKE TO BE THE SON OF AN UMPIRE?"

Fred Pryor has been asked that question many a time over the years. Here's a couple stories he relayed to answer the question...

My Tobacco Education

Sometime during the summer of 1962 I accompanied my dad on a road trip to St. Louis. I was nine years old. Big pops was in the second year umpiring in the big leagues. He was on a crew led by Augie Donatelli, which included veterans Frank Secory and Tony Venson. Before the game, I would hang out in the umpires' dressing room where there was always an abundance of sandwiches, soda and ice cream bars available. Nothing elaborate, just the essentials. I thought I was pretty fortunate to have access to all these "free treats" before the game and took full advantage! While preparing for the game, I noticed that Mr. Donatelli pulled a pouch out of his pocket, opened it, reached inside and pulled out some brown colored material, which he promptly packed in his mouth. I was not familiar with this brown substance so I inquired...

"Mr. Donatelli, what is that stuff you just put in your mouth?"

He replied, "It's chewin' tobacco Freddie, you wanna to try some?"

I was like, "yes sir... I'll give it a try!"

He looked at my dad and winked and handed me a plug. I said "Thanks Sir," and stuffed it in my pocket. I figured if it's served in the clubhouse it must be good like everything else right? I thought to myself... I'm gonna save this treat for later.

When the umpires got ready to take the field, I headed up to the stands and took my seat. After the managers and umpires at home plate, the ground rules discussions were completed, my dad would always look up the stands to make sure I had gotten to my seat okay before he took his position on the field. When he saw me, he'd give me "the Pez"... You know, tilt the head back as a sign of acknowledgment, like the Pez dispensers use to open when we were kids. Now, Big Pops always gave me a couple of bucks to spend during the game and I immediately sprang into action with my newfound wealth! I got hot dogs, Coke, some popcorn and my favorite, Frosty Malt (an ice cream treat popular at Wrigley Field in Chicago... St. Louis had their own version). This was all inhaled with great gusto by the end of the second inningwhich, by the way, was on top of the "pre-game" feeding frenzy that took place in the umpires' room prior to the game.

Then it occurred to me. I still had stuff, "the plug" Mr. Donatelli had given me. I dug in my pocket and pulled out the "crown jewel, of snacks! I wasn't sure what it was, but he had stuff quite a bit in his mouth, so it must be good, right? I put the entire plug in my mouth and began to chew with great vigor. Needless to say, the impact was immediate. A wave of nausea descended upon me like a swarm of locusts. I immediately knew I had to rid myself of this plague immediately. I made a direct beeline to the men's room and looked into the mirror and saw nothing but green! into the stall I went, where for the next seven or eight innings, I waged war with the offending "plug" and its accomplices: nausea, cold sweats, vomiting and "splashing shrapnel" damage.

After the game, I descended in the bowels of the stadium to go to the umpires' dressing room where I was greeted by my dad, along with the other umpires with looks of amazement and shock. I must have looked a mess by then. The offending "plug" had done its work well, wreaking havoc on my internal organs as well as my morale. I appeared to have gone through a blender on high speed! Splash shrapnel was still visible…in my hair, on my face. It was awful and it was everywhere. Professor Donatelli had administered his "tobacco education" with great skill and proficiency.

What's it like to be the son of an umpire you ask? Perilous.

Mr. Bill Jackowski

Bill Jackowski, from North Walpole, New Hampshire, was a National League umpire from 1952 to 1968. He had a storied career: Umpiring in three World Series and three All-Star games over 2,517 games in his 17-year tenure. He worked six no-hitters in his career, one being the Sandy Koufax perfect game on September 9, 1965. In that game, he umpired second base while my dad umpired third base. Coincidentally, this was Big Pops' second game of the day, having worked the day game in San Francisco to cover another umpire's emergency leave. He then flew back to Los Angeles for the night game. Two games, two different cities, one day.

Mr. Jackowski was also behind the plate in one of baseball's greatest games, Bill Mazeroski's game-winning home run in Game Seven of the 1960 World Series, which propelled the Pirates over the Yankees for the World Championship. He was a veteran baseball umpire, a man of distinction, always impeccably dressed with an unyielding faith in God. Mr. Jackowski, as my dad told me, attended Mass every day of the year. Every day of the year! I remember thinking to myself "this man was serious about his relationship with God and was not one to be trifled with."

In 1966, Big Pops was on the same crew with Bill Jackowski, John Kibler, and Ed Sudol. As I recall, Big Pops and I had driven down to Chicago from our home in Racine, Wisconsin as he was assigned to umpire the Cubs vs. Giants game later that afternoon. Racine was about an "hour and change" north of Chicago in 30 minutes south of Milwaukee, which is why Big Pops chose it as our home. Anytime he was assigned to games in Chicago and Milwaukee (home of the Braves at the time), he would spend time at home during the season. Big Moms got a well-deserved respite on those days he was a big fan of any kind of respite! Any relief…from raising kids by herself…right?

At the time, I was a big Willie Mays fan, so I was pulling for the Giants at the time. This was well before my conversion to the Pittsburgh Pirates. During the game, Bill Jackowski had made a call on the field regarding Willie Mays that, in my eyes, was unfavorable to Willie. Now, Big Pops that always told me to keep my ears and eyes open and my mouth shut when in the umpires' dressing. I'm not sure what compelled me, but after the game as the crowd noise had subsided, 12 year old little Freddie approached Mr. Bill Jackowski and asked him...

"Mr. Jackowski, I think you missed that call on Willie Mays. I thought he was safe...!?! You called his out, how come?"

The umpires' room got deathly silent, and judging by the "Detroit Death Stare" I was getting from Mr. Jackowski, I was quite sure I had entered the "Twilight Zone" from which there would be no return...

I think it was at that exact moment, Big Pops swallowed his cigar. Whole.

The other umpires'– Kibler and Sudol – eyes were wide open, looking like "startled Jackie Gleason's" as they observed the unfolding horror show.

Finally, after what seemed to be an eternity, Mr. Jackowski simply replied, "He. Was. Out." Period. End of discussion.

Followed by more silence.

At this point, Big Pops, having extracted the cigar from his throat, in just his fourth major league season and having his 12-year-old son question a call by... Mr. Bill Jackowski, a well-known and respected veteran umpire...quickly guided me into the shower room where he gave me the "cut it off" sign. You know, the "throat slash"... As in "shut up kid, you're killing me" signal!

Needless to say, I'll never forget Mr. Bill Jackowski, he was really an impressive figure who made a "significant impact" in my young life...he was in fact, a very nice, polite gentleman.

"Better to be seen and not heard in the clubhouse, right Big Pops?"

"That's right Freddie, seen and not heard… Ever!"

The ride home from Chicago to Racine seemed to last forever that evening…

Did You Wash Your Face and Brush Your Teeth?

During the off-season of baseball, my father was a teacher at St. Lucy's Parochial school in Racine, Wisconsin. In 1963, I was in fifth grade and used to walk to school with my classmates Dennis Goff and Tom Small. Of course I had the option of getting a ride to school with Big Pops, but the walk offered opportunities for a little freedom and adventure. We would often see Big Pops pass by us on Durand Avenue on his way to school. Then, thinking we were safe, we would resume whatever tomfoolery we were engaged in at the time. You know, innocent stuff right? Sure.

Every morning at the Pryor household, and I mean every morning before I left for school, Big Pops would ask me the following series of questions:

"Did you wash your face?"

"Yes, sir," I would reply.

"Did you use a facecloth?"

"Yes, sir," I replied.

"Did you brush your teeth?"

"Yes sir, I did."

What I would really do in most cases, would go into the bathroom, wet down my toothbrush and facecloth as if I had, in fact, actually used them when in most cases, I had not.

Now, you may ask, why didn't I just do what I was supposed to do? I don't know. Why do kids do or not do anything? Of course, I knew I was flirting with a potential confrontation with "The Beast," but hey, thrill seeker, let's push the edge of the envelope, right?

When Big Pops question me, my morning responses were always automatic:

"Yes sir, all done."

One particular winter day, we were walking to school down Durand Avenue, just in front of Wells Brothers Barbershop, when the big, blue Ford Galaxy 500 Big Pops drove pulled up next to us on the street and parked. All 6' 2", 250 pounds of Big Pops unfolded as he emerged from the car, leaving us over to him.

"I wonder, why is he stopping here?" I thought to myself unaware of the impending doom.

Not thinking anything was wrong; all three of us approached him, cautiously of course. He withdrew his large cigar from his mouth, which was producing its own billowing, smoking "ecological nightmare" resembling the steel mills of Pittsburgh in the 1930-40s, looked me over and asked me:

"Freddie, did you wash your face and brush your teeth this morning?"

A sense of panic swept over me...did I? Well did I? I had a mental lapse and honestly could not remember. The mere fact that he was there did not bode well for me. This could be a "Bad Day at Black Rock" I thought.

Auto response kicked in, and with great conviction I said, "Why yes, yes sir, I did."

Wrong answer. $%^#!

"Well then, why was your toothbrush facecloth bone dry when I checked?" replied Big Pops looming over me...

"Uhhhhh, Ummmmm, Ahhhh. Eeew. Iiiiii. Ooooooo." I went through all the vowels to no avail. "Not sure Dad...?!?

"Hmmmmm, well, since you can't seem to do it yourself, I guess I'll have to do it for you!" he replied.

Big Pops went into the front seat of his car, produced a wet, fully lathered soapy facecloth and proceeded with great vigor to "detail my face" right there on the sidewalk much to the shock and disbelief of my fellow classmates, Dennis and Tom, who by then, were slowly carefully backing away from the unfolding disaster!

After the face detailing was finished, he returned to the car, pulled out my toothbrush which was laden with toothpaste, and did a 360° fully comprehensive teeth cleaning in front of a now steadily increasing assemblage of St. Lucy's students who weren't quite sure what they were witnessing.

The carnage was complete. No rinse. No detail left uncovered. No jeans or Capri's please.

My face was intact and clean, and my teeth were brushed. I'm quite sure. Very sure.

He fired up his cigar, got back in his car and left the scene. Nothing else was ever said.

Big Pops had his own way of dealing with the young insurrectionist, Fred Pryor. It was swift and final... Not open to debate or interpretation. Direct and to the point. Public or private, it made no difference. There was no trifling with Big Pops. I had challenged "The Beast" and lost...

As time has unfolded, we all know those people who say they were there and personally witnessed Bill Mazeroski's World Series winning home run, Sandy Koufax's Perfect Game in Los Angeles, or Bart Starr's game-winning quarterback sneak against Dallas at Lambeau Field. If that was the fact, those stadium capacities must have been about three or four million apiece with all the people who said they were there, right?

"Oh sure, you betcha I was at that game!" they'd say. "Saw it with my own two eyes!"

Well, I still run into people from Racine, Wisconsin, whose to this day, claim they were on Durand Avenue in a cold, wintry morning, just across from Wells Brothers Barbershop in 1963, who personally witnessed "The Great Cleansing"!

"Oh sure, you betcha I was at that cleansing! Saw it with my own two eyes!"

Well, of this I'm 100% sure, I was there.

Without a doubt, it is one of my fondest memories of life growing up with Big Pops is my father. Crazy, right?

Big Pops loved me, and was not afraid to show the world how much he did!

Thanks Dad, I love you and thanks for caring so much!

Sorry I lied . Home

EPILOGUE: TRIBUTES TO PAUL PRYOR BY BOB CHICK AND JOSEPH A. SCOLARO

The following excerpt is from a tribute to Paul Pryor written shortly after his death on December 15, 1995, by *Tampa Tribune* columnist, Bob Chick:

Former NL ump Pryor remembered for his hard work

The essence of Paul Pryor likely could be seen in the simplest of acts.

It was nothing, really. He took three hours out of a Saturday in February 1994 to umpire a fundraising benefit for Chantelle Rivera, the cancer-stricken young daughter of former major leaguer Bombo Rivera.

And you don't even have to think about all the times he picked up the same older man along the road who walked everywhere he went. "Get in," Pryor use to command in a heavy voice. "I'll take you where you want to go."

Those weren't good deeds, he probably would say. Just daily living. He never stopped working nor did he stop giving…

A massive stroke cut him down two weeks after he umpired that benefit game at Al Lang Stadium. They didn't expect him to make it through the crucial hours that followed. He lasted another 21 months, a second stroke and several major infections. Four times doctors said he wouldn't last the night. Four times his son, Fred, was prepared to fly in from his home in Dallas…Nothing was easy since the stroke. He lost most of his ability to speak and couldn't get around without help.

A common man, it could be said, cast in the spotlight. For 20 years he was a National League umpire. Identification went with the position, but he was just as close with cabdrivers, porters, clubhouse attendants, and ushers. "He was just one of the boys," Fred Pryor said Sunday evening at a St. Petersburg restaurant.

One of the guys had a face like a leatherneck Marine, as rough and as snarled as an old oak. He could take down a cigar until the final ash danced on his lips. His drink was Scotch on the rocks. "One of the guys" was all meat and potatoes. 260 pounds pressed over a 6'2" body.

Slow down, he was told. "When I'm dead, I'll get all the rest I need," he would say. It wasn't a perfect retort, but you couldn't expect perfection out of someone whose wardrobe looked like a consignment shop clearance.

Fred Pryor greeted his dad one day in the Dallas airport when he arrived with brown shoes, maroon socks, khaki pants, maroon belt, green and black checkered jacket, a tie as wide as a hand towel, and a blue umpire's shirt.

It was called dressing up. Fred worked for Delta and Dad was told to conform to a respectable dress code.

Yet there was more to the man than the face and the clothes. He had been a minor league ballplayer, later an umpire, teacher and a principal. He had been a football and basketball coach. And a businessman and owner of Paul Pryor Travel Bags. He was a handshake from everyone in baseball.

Everything was right with Fred and his dad, though it had been a bit rocky when he was a youngster. Fred found it was okay to be Fred and didn't have to fill his dad's shoes.

"There was not a lot of touchy-feely, I-love-you type of things in our family," Fred said. "But my folks know I love them. I cried a lot this weekend. I laughed a lot. I can think of so many of the good things."

So much of it was baseball and sports and education. Fred Pryor was once a pupil in his dad's history class at St. Lucy's in Racine, Wisconsin. Dad paddled everyone one day when the eighth grade boys got into a lunchroom to fight with peas against the seventh-graders. Fred got three whacks, everyone else one.

The son laughs about it. A few tears also get an airing when the son talks about his wedding and how much fun his dad had during that time in New Orleans. Those are the things that last. "He was a neat guy, that's all," said his son. That, too, was to be remembered. Home

The following tribute to Paul Pryor was written by *Racine Journal Times* columnist Joseph A. Scolaro, shortly following Pryor's death on December 15, 1995 (reprinted with permission from the *Racine Journal Times*):

NL umpire ex-Racinian Pryor dies

Paul Pryor will be remembered as a kind of person who could make anybody feel special.

Pryor, the former National League baseball umpire who lived in Racine in the 1960s, died Friday at St. Petersburg Florida.

Pryor, 68, died after suffering a stroke at a nursing home. Pryor had suffered a series of strokes recently.

"He was very much liked, respected by everyone in the community," Pryor's son, Fred, said Saturday in a telephone interview from Florida. "He did a lot of work for kids. He did a lot of public speaking. He was one of those nobody felt uncomfortable around."

Pryor lived in Racine from the early 1960's to the mid-1970's and taught at St. Lucy's school. Pryor was born in Woonsocket, Rhode Island. He chose to live in Racine because of its location between Milwaukee and Chicago. As an umpire, Pryor traveled much during the summers, but could visit his family in Racine if he was working in Milwaukee Braves game or Chicago Cubs game, Fred said. The 6'2" 225 pound Pryor played minor league baseball but never made it to the majors before injuries forced him to quit. He managed in the minor leagues and got into umpiring quite literally by accident.

In 1948, an umpire in the Georgia State League was injured in an accident. Pryor was asked to fill in and wound up finishing the season.

Following his graduation from High Point, North Carolina College, Pryor returned to umpiring in 1954. On September 1, 1961, the National League purchased Pryor's contract from the American Association. He worked his first major league game on September 22 – a Pirates-Phillies game at Philadelphia's Connie Mack Stadium.

Pryor umpired the World Series in 1967, 1973 and 1980, worked the All-Star game in 1963, 1971, 1978, and umpired the playoffs in 1970, 1974, 1977 and 1981.

When Pryor umpired in the major leagues, the men in blue preferred staying in the background. But confrontations have escalated, Pryor said several years ago, and not just because of the players.

"Some of these umpires have to have the last word," he said at the time. "They're laying a trap so to speak. A lot of times these young umpires will follow a player yelling, 'What did you say?' Naturally, the player's going to turn around and then you've got a shouting match going and the umpire runs him."

When he lived in Racine, Pryor taught history and social studies at St. Lucy's School and was active in the school's athletic program. He was a well-known public speaker in the Racine area and started a basketball program at Dominican College, where he was the college's first basketball coach for several years. Fred said his father's favorite hangouts included Devine's Sporting Goods Store, De Mark Brothers Tavern, and Wells Brothers Bar and Restaurant.

"He liked our food," Guy Wells said. "Every time he stopped by, he would bring some baseballs. He was a very good man. An outstanding individual."

Wells said Pryor brought umpires from Kenosha's minor league games to the restaurant, and sometimes a famous player, such as Ernie Banks from the Chicago Cubs, who enjoyed a homemade wine made by an uncle of Guy Wells.

Fred said his father knew many people, from big sports stars to baseball stadium ground crew members.

"He had a vast, vast network of people from sports and all walks of life," Fred Pryor said. "He always seemed like he took special time for everybody. He didn't have to be a big star. He hung out with the regular guys. That was back in the day when umpires chose to be less flamboyant." *The Associated Press also contributed to this story.* Home

APPENDIX I

Facebook Post written For *Old Time Baseball Photos* by Gary Livacari, December 16, 2016

Fred Pryor's Reminiscences of His Father

"I hear you're Paul Pryor's son, huh? I knew your old man when I played ball back in South Dakota, back in the late '40's or so…. He was a helluva guy!"

As we've mentioned numerous times, we always love it when we're contacted by relatives of former ball players. But today we've got something just a little bit different. Recently we were contacted by Fred Pryor, son of Paul Pryor who umpired in the National League for 21 years (1961-1981). I'm sure our "senior" readers will recognize his name, along with other members of his crew from the early 1960's: Frank Secory, Ed Sudol, and Ken Burkhart.

Fred Pryor describes his father as "one of a kind," to which the above quote testifies. Not only was he an outstanding umpire, an accomplished public speaker, and later, a successful business man, he was also a devoted husband and father of four who tried to balance all of the many demands placed upon him by his career and personal life. Before his start in umpiring, Paul Pryor was a minor league baseball pitcher from 1945 to 1948. He became interested in umpiring while attending college in the late 1940's, seeing it as a way to make extra money. After graduation and starting out on his career as a baseball and football coach, he continued umpiring on the side. Soon after, he landed jobs in the minor leagues and was encouraged by "baseball people" that umpiring was something he should pursue. He went to spring training one year and made a favorable impression and finally made it to the "Big Show" in September 1961.

Fred Pryor is understandably proud of his dad, who he fondly refers to as "Big Pops." Over his career, the Woonsocket, Rhode Island native umpired 3,094 major league games, including three World Series, four League Championship series, and three All-Star games. Pryor's crew had many memorable games, including one on May 31, 1964 that went 23 innings. The second game of a double header, it's the longest doubleheader in National League history, with the crew officiating 33 innings that day. They also called Jim Bunning's Perfect Game on June 21, 1964, one of only 23 official Perfect Games in major league history. I asked Fred if he'd share a few reminisces about what it was like being the son of a major league umpire. He willingly responded with some interesting information:

Fred has cherished memories from those days when his dad was on the major league circuit. Because Big Pops "knew just about everyone in baseball," Fred got an insiders' view of the game not available to other kids. His dad introduced him to players, coaches, front office personnel, grounds crews, clubhouse attendants, vendors, cops outside the park, firemen in the station across the street, and even bartenders at favorite umpire "watering holes." Fred also shared with me his dad's beautiful philosophy of life: "Everyone has value, everyone matters. Never treat someone any better just because he makes more money or has an important title. Everyone counts.

There are no ordinary people." Above all, Fred added, Big Pops started out his career as a teacher and coach, and his respect for the profession stayed with him for the rest of his life. Paul Pryor never stopped teaching.

Because of his Dad's vast sports connections, Fred's experiences extended into other sports besides baseball. Once in 1969 or '70, when the Vikings were playing the Packers in Milwaukee, Paul Pryor used his connection with the County Stadium clubhouse attendant and his friendship with some of the Viking players to get his son and his buddies into the Vikings' clubhouse. It was an experience they never forgot, as they met many Vikings players. Fred even got a signed ball from center Mick Tinglehoff. Another time Fred got to meet the Packers' great quarterback Bart Starr at a Father and Son banquet in which Paul Pryor was the Master of Ceremonies. The baseball players Fred met would make any of us envious, including Roberto Clemente, Willie Stargell, Manny Sanguillen, Stan Musial, Pete Rose, Ernie Banks, Willie Mays, Mike Schmidt, and Billy Williams. Being the son of a well-known major league umpire definitely had its advantages!

Fred recalled that his family moved to Racine, Wisconsin when he was in fourth grade. Big Pops would come home during the season whenever the Cubs played the Braves. Fred's mother Carleen greatly appreciated this rare opportunity to see her husband during the long baseball season. Reflecting on the demanding role of an umpire's wife, Fred added: "Try raising four kids by yourself seven months a year with no relief…It's definitely not fun!"

When Paul Pryor was umpiring the 1973 World Series, Fred went with some friends after work to a local bar to watch the game. After the National Anthem was played and the players and umpires were being introduced, the cameras panned the infield. Fred saw his dad on center stage on national television. He recalled how proud he was: "Wow…that's actually Big Pops up there!" It's an image he never forgot.

A respected umpire known to have a "thick skin," Paul Pryor recorded only 30 ejections over his career, including one stretch of nearly five years without a single one. He was very familiar with the hazards of the game, once suffering broken teeth from a Willie Stargell foul ball that caught him square in the mask. Pryor maintained his teaching and coaching positions during the off-seasons, and worked at various times as a car salesman, a football referee, a beer salesman, and as an in-demand public speaker. He retired from umpiring in 1981 after on-going struggles with foot problems.

In the 1970's, Paul Pryor designed a duffel bag for umpire equipment. The idea caught on, and soon "Paul Pryor Travel Bags" were on the market. At one time the company had accounts with the NCAA, Major League Baseball, the National Football League, the Canadian Football League, plus many schools and businesses.

Paul Pryor, affectionately known to his family as "Big Pops," passed away on December 15, 1995, aged 68, while residing in St. Petersburg, Florida. Home

APPENDIX II:

"The Paul Pryor Effect," by Fred Pryor

Wrigley Field

There used to be a man named Dick who ran the umpires clubhouse at Wrigley Field. I cannot remember his last name. I'm not sure I ever knew it to begin with, I just knew him as Dick. He had a great personality and always seemed very upbeat. The umpires treated him very well to my knowledge. Dick also ran the referee's clubhouse for the NFL as the Bears used to play their home games at Wrigley.

In the winter of 1963, the Bears and the New York Giants were meeting at Wrigley for the NFL Championship Game. Big Pops decided we should take a ride from Racine down to Chicago to catch this game so he gave Dick a call. In true Dick fashion, he said "Sure, come on down...I can't get tickets for seats as the game is sold out, but I can get you inside the park." Well, that was all Big Pops needed to hear. He called up a restaurant buddy of his, last name was Larson, and invited him and his son to accompany us to the game. When we got to Wrigley, Big Pops stuck his head in the clubhouse to tell Dick thanks and to greet the NFL referees, some of which he knew. We then headed up by the scoreboard where we found a great place to stand and watch the game.

It was the coldest day that I ever experienced in my life. But hey, it was the NFL Championship; I was ten years old and on top of the world. I think I finally thawed out about the time we arrived back in Racine later that night.

Dick also got us ground crew passes for another game at Wrigley in 1970-71 as the Bears were hosting the Green Bay Packers. The ground crew passes allowed us to have access to the sidelines during the game as long as we stayed around the 20-25 yard line and stayed out of the players' way. Now, in those days, both teams shared the same sidelines at Wrigley so we roamed behind both benches, spending most of the first half on the Bear's end of the field. After the half, we moved to the Packer's end of the field and took in the action from that vantage point. I had asked a high school buddy, Rick Naleid, to go to the game with me. We both had our J.I. Case high school letterman's jackets on so our friends and families could see us on T.V. should we be so lucky. Right?

Now Rule #1 on standing on the sidelines is: Never take your eyes off the action. Never. If a play is headed towards you, back up "most rickey tick" to avoid disaster. In other words, get out of the way RIGHT NOW! Earlier, I had advised Rickey about Rule #1 prior to the game, so when Green Bay ran a sweep towards our sideline with Guard Gale Gillingham leading the way for RB Travis Williams, I sensed a collision was forthcoming. The Bears defense was also heading in our direction with malice in their eyes...Linebacker's Doug Buffone, Dick Butkus et al.

Both Big Pops and I began backpedaling furiously away from the sideline but Rickey Boy was frozen in his shoes as the play unfolded before his eyes. Tons of humanity converged directly upon Rickey as the Bears defenders collided with the Packers offensive thrust. It was a cold and rainy that day at Wrigley as the players began to un-pile. LB Doug Buffone reached down and pulled 145 lb. Rick up from the quagmire. As Rickey was helped to his feet, he raised both arms over his head like Rocky Balboa screaming he had made the play! "Where are the T.V. cameras pointing….am I on T.V.?!?" It was hilarious. Big Pops just shook his head side to side and took another puff from his cigar. Rickey Boy still tells the story how he took on both NFL teams and lived to tell about it.

Milwaukee County Stadium

One Sunday, Big Pops, my high school quarterback, Ralph Porcaro and I went to County Stadium to see the Packers play the Minnesota Vikings the year they played in Super Bowl III. Longtime visiting team and umpire clubhouse manager, Jim Ksicinski, had played basketball for my dad back in the late 1960's at Dominican College in Racine, Wisconsin, so we stopped in after the game to say hello. My dad knew some of the NFL referees and was buddies with Vikings Center Mick Tinglehoff. This was the era of the "Purple People Eaters," and needless to say Ralph and I were both in awe as we were led around the room by Mick and introduced to the Vikings players. He gave us a couple of Viking t-shirts; you would have thought we won the lottery! An experience Ralph and I will never forget.

Three Rivers Stadium

I went to Pittsburgh in August of 1979 for a weekend series with the Pirates vs. Phillies who were battling for the lead in the division at the time. I've been a Pirates fan since I was a kid living in Puerto Rico, so I was pumped up for this five game series. They had a double-header on Friday, a single game Saturday, and another double-header on Sunday. I was working for Delta Air Lines in Chicago and had flown to Pittsburgh for these games which I had circled on the calendar as soon as I found out Big Pops was working this series. The Bucs swept the series and never looked back going on to win the World Series that year!

Before the first game, I was in the clubhouse with all the umpires and my dad said "Follow me, someone wants to meet you." So I followed him into the hallway and lo and behold, motioning to me down the hallway from the Pirates clubhouse was Bucs' manager Chuck Tanner. He invited me into his office and we talked baseball for about twenty minutes. Then he brought me into the Pirates clubhouse and introduced me to Manny Sanguillen, Willie Stargell, Dave Parker and several other Bucs. I was speechless and overwhelmed. After that, my Dad and I went into the Phillies' dugout and were surrounded by Pete Rose, Bob Boone and Greg Luzinski. We chatted for a few minutes as other Phillies players passed by.

I'll never forget that weekend spending time with Big Pops, the Pirates…seizing first place and never looking back!

I always tell my wife my life was "front end loaded". I was so very fortunate to be exposed to all these great sports venues and personalities when I was a kid…all of which were made possible by my father, Big Pops. He never met a stranger and all throughout my life people would say "So your Paul's kid huh? I knew your old man playing ball back in "so in so" in '48…helluva guy that old man of yours is, kid!"

They had that right…one helluva guy indeed! Home

ABOUT THE AUTHORS

Fred Pryor

Fred Pryor spent sixteen years with Delta Air Lines in passenger service, ten years in the fitness industry, and nine years with GameStop Inc., being in leadership the majority of his working career. He's strongly believes in the credo: People that feel good about themselves and what they are doing will generally produce good results! Fred's leadership philosophy is simple: "Anyone can point out things that people do wrong, that's easy. Try finding the things people are doing right and illuminate it for all to see. That's leadership! Elevation of the spirit is paramount!" Fred currently does leadership and motivational work for individuals and groups in the D/FW area. His wife of 32 years Tricia is retired from Delta Air Lines after 30 years of service as a flight attendant. She is unquestionably the foundation of the Pryor family! She is an outstanding wife and mother.

Fred and Tricia have two sons: John Paul, and Samuel Brady. Paul is also in leadership in the insurance industry. He is making great strides developing his skills and broadening his career opportunities. Sam is a Special Olympian and lives in a group home with five other special needs gentlemen.

Fred can be contacted at: prymontre@gmail.com

Gary Livacari

Baseball historian Gary Livacari is a long-time member of the Society for Baseball Research (SABR) who enjoys writing about baseball. His forte is identifying ball players in old photos. For many years he did player identifications for the Baseball Fever web site. He was also an editor for the Boston Public Library Leslie Jones Baseball Project, helping to identify ball players in almost 3000 photos from the 1930s and 1940s. He has written biographies for the SABR Bioproject, plus numerous articles and book reviews. His latest book, *Memorable World Series Moments*, was published last October and is available on Amazon.

He is the co-editor of the *Old Time Baseball Photos* Facebook page, which has grown to over 73,000 followers; and he is also the developer and administrator of the *Baseball History Comes Alive!* web page, which also enjoys a large following.

Gary and his wife Nancy have been married for 40 years. They have two children and four grandchildren. He can be contacted at: Livac2@aol.com Home

Made in the USA
Lexington, KY
23 May 2018